D0428724

The Alexis de Tocqueville
Lectures on American Politics

Obama and America's Political Future

Theda Skocpol

WITH COMMENTARIES BY
Larry M. Bartels
Mickey Edwards
Suzanne Mettler

HARVARD UNIVERSITY PRESS
Cambridge, Massachusetts
London, England
2012

Library of Congress Cataloging-in-Publication Data

Skocpol, Theda.
Obama and America's political future / Theda Skocpol ;
with commentaries by Larry M. Bartels, Mickey
Edwards, and Suzanne Mettler.
pages   cm.—(Alexis de Tocqueville lectures on
American politics)
Includes bibliographical references and index.
ISBN 978-0-674-06597-0 (alk. paper)
1. United States—Politics and government—2009–
2. Obama, Barack.   3. Tea Party movement.
I. Bartels, Larry M., 1956–   II. Edwards, Mickey, 1937–
III. Mettler, Suzanne.   IV. Title.
E907.S6   2012
973.932—dc23   2012003663

CONTENTS

FOREWORD

IN POLITICS, HISTORIC AND UNEXPECTED UPHEAVALS CAN
deliver lessons rich in their variety and texture. The broad
electoral victories of President Barack Obama and Democratic congressional candidates in 2008, followed by similarly expansive triumphs for Republican legislative candidates in 2010, were predictable in the narrow sense—the
first occurring in the midst of a massive economic downturn
and an unpopular incumbent president, the second occurring in a midterm election in which the new incumbent had
himself become unpopular. Yet judging from the vantage of
policy change and from the longer term, the results do not
arrive at so easy an account. With Republican operative Karl
Rove publicly envisioning a "permanent Republican majority" after the reelection of President George W. Bush in 2004,
who would have predicted the stunning turnabout of 2008,
which produced not only robust Democratic majorities but
also a range of major legislative enactments? And with journalists claiming that the nation was in the midst of a "new"
New Deal, who could have predicted the size of the Republicans' victories in 2010?

In her Alexis de Tocqueville Lecture in American Politics,
Professor Theda Skocpol takes the Obama presidency and

sets it in the dynamic context of American political development. Skocpol has long been a pioneer in the analysis of global political history and American political development in particular. In her recent work she helps lead an international effort to bring historically informed social science to the study of contemporary political developments. Here she asks what became of the "new" New Deal the Obama presidency had promised and what this past history augurs for the future.

The lecture displays Professor Skocpol's classic and highly influential style of analysis, a style that avoids a "timeless political science," bringing context and contingency squarely into the analysis. She offers useful and unprecedented comparisons of the early Obama years with the FDR era and with the presidencies of Lyndon Baines Johnson, Jimmy Carter, and Ronald Reagan. The scope, power, and originality of these comparisons are an impressive feat, especially given how much journalistic and academic ink has been spilled on the Obama presidency to date. She then offers us a new portrait of the Tea Party, based in part upon her pathbreaking work with Harvard graduate student Vanessa Williamson—drawing upon deep quantitative and qualitative analysis of media coverage, voting patterns, Tea Party organizations, and hundreds of hours of interviews across the country. She concludes with a bold look to the future, once again focusing less on hasty predictions regarding the next election and more on broad and penetrating insight into the longer-term developments in American politics and social policy.

Three skilled critics offer their reactions, and the result is a fascinating exchange regarding historical antecedents, theoretical perspectives, and statistical patterns. Vanderbilt

Professor Larry Bartels, probably the top scholarly analyst of American elections working today, puzzles over whether recent electoral swings represent a contingent development or a continuation of durable patterns in American electoral behavior, and he questions the efficacy of a presidential bully pulpit. Mickey Edwards, longtime Republican congressman from Oklahoma and an astute observer of the American political scene, examines the purported mandate of the early Obama years in light of Republican efforts to claim mandates for their own policies. Cornell political scientist Suzanne Mettler, who with scholars like Jacob Hacker and Paul Pierson stands at the head of the new political science analysis of policy development, asks what it is about the structure of America's emerging policy state that makes policy change and political change more taxing, and which makes any reform-oriented presidency's tasks so daunting. Displaying respect and combat-readiness to her critics, Professor Skocpol concludes the volume with her rebuttals. She defends an approach that weds historical contingency and timing to political change, and she reflects anew about what current policy and electoral developments might or might not last.

What results from this exchange is, I am confident, the best treatment yet in print of the first two years of the Obama presidency and the Tea Party–fueled Republican resurgence. These two intertwined developments will be chronicled and analyzed for decades to come. Yet those accounts will have to begin with the masterful narrative provided in Professor Skocpol's lecture, with the exchange that follows it, and with the cogent summary of historical developments, theoretical insight, and macroanalysis provided in the volume.

Professor Skocpol's lecture was delivered as part of the Alexis de Tocqueville Lectures in American Politics, organized and sponsored by the Center for American Political Studies (CAPS) at Harvard. Every Tocqueville lecture depends upon organizational and financial resources for sustenance. I wish to thank the dean of the Faculty of Arts and Sciences, Michael D. Smith, and the deans of the Social Sciences in recent years, David Cutler, Stephen Kosslyn, and now Peter Marsden. I want to acknowledge, in particular, the generosity of Terry and Betsy Considine and the Donald T. Regan Lecture Fund. I also want to acknowledge an array of Harvard teachers and scholars whose support of the Tocqueville Lectures has been critical to their success: Sven Beckert, Lizabeth Cohen, Claudine Gay, Jennifer Hochschild, Harvey Mansfield, Lisa McGirr, Nancy Rosenblum, and Mary Waters. Lilia Halpern-Smith, the assistant director of CAPS, has efficiently organized every Tocqueville Lecture since the inaugural event. She provides wisdom and leadership for the center's many communities and publics, and with our colleague Abigail Peck she delivers welcoming, kind, and effective service that sustains the importance of those critical details that make an event like this a success. Lilia and Abby have my deep gratitude for work without which this event and book would not appear as they do. Joyce Seltzer of Harvard University Press did her usual superb job of taking a set of manuscripts from their inception through multiple drafts to the finished form of an academic publication—all with a professionalism for which I and all the authors are very grateful.

My final thanks go to Larry, Mickey, Suzanne, and Theda herself. I remember that March evening with gratitude, and as I read over the lecture and the ensuing debate, I count myself fortunate to have been a listener and reader of the evening's exchanges.

Daniel Carpenter
Director, Center for American Political Studies
Harvard University

Obama and
America's Political Future

1

OBAMA'S NEW DEAL, TEA PARTY REACTION, AND AMERICA'S POLITICAL FUTURE

Theda Skocpol

J UST WEEKS AFTER THE 2008 ELECTION, THE COVER OF the November 24, 2008, issue of *Time* magazine featured a broadly grinning Barack Obama wearing a fedora and riding FDR-style in an open convertible car, a cigarette in a long silver holder jutting from his lips. Entitled "The *New* New Deal—What Barack Obama Can Learn from F.D.R.—and What Democrats Need to Do," the magazine's feature stories explained how newly elected President Obama might propel a shift in U.S. governance and politics comparable to Franklin Delano Roosevelt's first New Deal in the 1930s. The stars were aligned, the *Time* authors suggested, for the incoming Obama administration, backed by robust Democratic majorities in Congress, to fashion public programs and tax measures that would help a majority of Americans—and do so in a way that could cement Democrats in their majority for years to come.[1]

Time might have been a bit over the top, but many pundits at the time agreed that momentum in U.S. politics lay with the Democrats. After all, the new Democratic president-elect was smart, eloquent, and very popular, backed by a broad, cross-regional, and multiracial coalition dominated by voters under age 45. Amid unpopular wars and a deepening economic downturn, most Americans seemed to be looking to Obama and Washington for "change you can believe in." By contrast, Republicans were stung not just by the presidential loss but also by huge setbacks in Congress and statehouses; they were also hampered by the broad unpopularity of outgoing GOP president George W. Bush. Reduced to a hard core centered in the once-Confederate South and the inner West, Republicans were virtually written off by many commentators in late 2008. Obama and the Democrats appeared to enjoy an extraordinary opportunity to use federal government power to counter the economic downturn and begin to reverse the increased inequality and spreading social insecurities of recent decades. If Obama Democrats could fashion a second New Deal, perhaps political good fortune would smile for some time on the new president's party.

How fast electoral fortunes—and pundit prognostications—can turn around. Obama's popularity declined only months into his presidency, and by the fall of 2009 substantial majorities questioned his economic stewardship. More telling, Democratic congressional fortunes took what turned out to be a portentous turn for the worse as early as January 2010, when a special Senate election in Massachusetts to fill the seat of recently deceased liberal lion Ted Kennedy shockingly resulted in victory for a conservative Republican backed by populist protesters in the Tea Party. Nine and a half months later, gale-force winds hit Democrats as Barack Obama's party experienced defeats of epic proportions in the November 2010 elections. Sixty-three seats switched from Democrats to Republicans in the House of Representatives, forcing the Democratic speaker of the 111th House, Nancy Pelosi, to hand the gavel to GOP speaker John Boehner just after noon on Wednesday, January 5, 2011. Of equal if not greater significance, the 2010 elections changed party fortunes in the states, as Republicans won 23 out of 37 gubernatorial races, and now control 30 out of 50 statehouses.[2] Republicans also made huge gains in state legislatures, and now hold full sway in legislatures plus governorships in seventeen states. This happened just prior to redistricting decisions following the 2010 census that would tip further the Republican way because of such state-level gains. For Democrats losses in the electorally pivotal region of the Midwest were especially worrisome. The GOP is no longer bottled up in the old South plus the inner West; now the party holds sway in states such as Florida, Michigan, Ohio, and Wisconsin, which are keys to Barack Obama's bid for reelection in 2012.

Did the huge 2008 to 2010 turnaround back toward the Republicans happen because President Obama and the Democrats failed to deliver on their major campaign promises made during 2007 and 2008? It would be hard to reach such a conclusion because the record of policy accomplishments and promises fulfilled was impressive.[3] President Obama and the Democrats of the 111th Congress fashioned landmark pieces of legislation for comprehensive health reform, the revamping of higher educational loans, and the regulation of Wall Street financial practices. The Obama administration used cabinet powers to spur school reforms, improve health and safety enforcement, enforce immigration laws, and tackle environmental threats. Economists of various persuasions and the nonpartisan Congressional Budget Office agree that the fledgling Obama administration and congressional majorities also took the basic steps necessary in 2009 to cut short a financial crisis, prevent the sudden disappearance of the U.S. auto industry, and forestall overall economic collapse into a second Great Depression. During 2009 and 2010, America's beleaguered economy turned from nearly unprecedented contraction to gradual growth.[4] All this happened as the White House pulled back from the protracted bloodletting in Iraq and, as Obama had promised during the 2008 campaign, redoubled the military effort in Afghanistan in preparation for starting a pullback in 2011.

Big policy accomplishments there may have been, but the projected political payoffs for Democrats certainly did not materialize. Leading into the fall 2010 elections, the economy remained in the doldrums and unemployment was close to 10 percent. In this dire economic situation, Obama's early presidency was not only proclaimed a failure by his opponents but also deemed a disappointment by many of his initial supporters.[5] The House of Representatives shifted to GOP control and shifted markedly toward the ideological far right. Republicans who took office in 2011 smelled blood. GOP leaders declared their determination to block any further Democratic initiatives, roll back public spending to the level of 2008 before Obama took office, and repeal or eviscerate the Democrats' early signature accomplishment, the Patient Protection and Affordable Care Act of 2010. Indeed, as its first big move in 2011, the GOP House changed budget scoring rules and limited amendments and debate in order to rush forward quickly with a full repeal vote on health reform, taking this aggressive step even before President Obama could deliver his next State of the Union Address in front of the newly seated 112th Congress. Thereafter, Republicans in Congress—and in many key states as well—embarked on unending legislative guerrilla warfare against Obama and

Democratic programs and priorities. Erase the Obama era altogether! That, in essence, was the rallying cry of the Republicans after their 2010 rebound.

Far from the advent of sustained Democratic dominance, in short, the early Obama presidency gave way to conservative backlash. And the GOP electoral rebound may continue. Because there are 23 Democratic Senate seats at stake in 2012, compared to only 10 currently held by Republicans, the GOP may capture a Senate majority, while it will be difficult for Democrats to reclaim the House in 2012. Obama may or may not be defeated in a 2012 GOP bid for full control of all branches of the federal government. But GOP primary contests to see who wins the opportunity to try to make Obama a one-term president, followed by a high-stakes presidential contest, will keep right-wing priorities front and center on the national political agenda through 2012 and beyond.

The startling turnarounds of recent U.S. politics—from a change election in 2008 to another switcheroo in 2010—raise fundamental questions. The pages that follow explore three sets of issues and suggest answers or possibilities, to the extent possible in dealing with ongoing events.

What happened to that "*new* New Deal" predicted for Obama and the Democrats? This is the first question, already posed. Fresh policymaking may merit the label, but the political results were not as expected, for several reasons. During his first two years, Obama had to deal with a sudden financial and economic meltdown, and did so in ways that looked like a betrayal to many Americans worried about loss of savings, livelihoods, and jobs. Although Democrats seemed to be "in charge" in Washington, D.C., legislative achievements came slowly and with messy, controversial political bargains that looked highly partisan. Given current media dynamics and presidential choices, policy developments and shortfalls were never well explained to citizens, leaving them angry or anxious amid the continuing economic crisis. Most achievements by Obama and the Democrats were invisible or worrisome to supporters, yet provocative and threatening to opponents. Politically, it was the worst combination—leading to friends who stood down while enemies mobilized.

Mention of opponents reminds us that the story of 2009 and 2010 was not just about Democrats in Washington. It was also about an explosive Tea Party that refocused and reshaped the GOP. We have to ask not only why Republicans rebounded—a certain amount of that was always in the cards for 2010—but why the party hurtled toward the far right and adopted an increasingly fierce and rigid antigovernment stance. Parties usually make gains through moderation, but the exact opposite happened in this case. I will dissect the popular and elite components of the Tea Party reaction to Obama's presidency that helped to reposition the Republican Party in ways likely to reverberate for years to come.

Finally, after I probe Obama's "halfway New Deal," and assess the whys and wherefores of the GOP's lunge toward the right, we will look ahead. In an era of major, inescapable national challenges, where is U.S. politics headed next? What do the crosswinds of political changes of the past few years portend for the vitality of our democracy and the effectiveness of our governance?

Obama's Halfway New Deal

In a number of ways, the November 2008 election seemed to open the door to more than incremental shifts in U.S. policy and politics. Most presidential contests after 1988 had culminated in plurality victories or very close outcomes, but Barack Obama won decisively—especially for a Democrat in recent memory. Obama's margin over John McCain was 53 percent to 46 percent in the total popular vote, and 365 to 173 in the Electoral College. At the same time, congressional Democrats strengthened their majorities in both the House and the Senate—and midway through 2009, when the protracted court battles in Minnesota were finally settled, the 58 Democrats plus 2 Independents in the Senate Democratic caucus gained some possibility of overcoming GOP filibusters.

The U.S. elections of 2006 and 2008 were also marked by the mobilization of new blocs of voters into greater participation, as well as enhanced support for the Democratic Party. Younger voters raised their level of engagement; African Americans turned out in droves to vote for the first African American presidential candidate; and Latino voters increased their level of participation and shifted toward a greater margin of support for Democrats.[6] Around the November 2008 election, commentators especially noted the age-gradient of partisan divisions, and trumpeted the Democratic Party, preferred by under-45-year-olds, as the party of the future.[7]

Barack Obama won the presidency at a juncture when most Americans of all political persuasions were disillusioned with his predecessor, George W. Bush, and the policies Bush had pursued with GOP support. To reach the White House backed by congressional party majorities after the country has "repudiated" the predecessors bodes well for an ambitious president determined to change policy directions.[8] In addition, some analysts would say that it is good for a president who wants to use federal power vigorously to come to office during a deep economic downturn, with businesses and average citizens open to a helping hand from government.[9] Barack Obama arrived in Washington just as an epochal financial meltdown was plunging the country into the Great Recession, the deepest economic downturn since the 1930s.

Finally, Obama made no secret that he would seek to change the direction of federal social and fiscal policies. During the 2007 primaries and the 2008 general election, Obama promised to help average Americans and argued that prosperous families, making more than $250,000 a year, should pay higher taxes. Candidate Obama called for growth and economic renewal "from the bottom up" rather than the top down, aiming to reinvigorate the American middle class and broaden its ranks.[10] Obama's pledges to change direction followed years of federal policies that had redistributed wealth upward, while reducing taxes on the very rich and eliminating many regulatory limits on business.[11]

THE CHALLENGE OF REALIZING CHANGE

Even at the height of speculation about a possible New Deal, analysts sounded notes of caution and pointed toward predictable roadblocks. U.S. electoral outcomes normally swing back and forth—and a rebound for the out-party is especially likely in midterm congressional elections when the other party controls the presidency and both houses of Congress. FDR's 1936 landslide was followed by midterm losses of 71 seats in the House and half a dozen in the Senate; Lyndon

Johnson's Democratic Party lost 47 House seats two years after its landslide win in 1964. In general, the party in power has lost 22 seats in the House since World War II, and the losses have been higher when presidential approval ratings slipped below 50 percent (as was the case for Obama during 2010). In general, older, richer, and whiter voters are the ones most likely to turn out in midterm elections—and according to exit polling for the 2008 election, these were the demographics least enamored of Barack Obama.[12] Savvy analysts knew from the start—and so did Democratic Party strategists—that the president and his congressional copartisans would likely face electoral setbacks in 2010.

Beyond normal electoral swings, it has long been well documented in survey research that Americans are ideologically cautious about strong government or governmental activism. From the very beginning of mass surveys and continuing until the present, researchers have noted that if you ask Americans abstract questions—such as "Do you agree that people in government waste a lot of money we pay in taxes?"—they favor the free market and oppose government intervention; but if you ask them about specifics—such as "Do you support Social Security?" or "Would you be willing to pay more taxes for early childhood education?"—they tend to support liberal positions about active government.[13] Americans are, in short, philosophical conservatives and operational liberals. This means that even if Americans approve many specific measures furthered by President Obama and the Democrats, popular worries could be stoked by political opponents. As a young, change-oriented president, Obama would have faced such worries under any circumstances. But the spreading economic distress of 2009 and 2010 generated genuine fear that was readily exploited by political foes who equated even mild government activism with "radicalism."

The divisions inherent in a large congressional majority would also predictably bedevil the Obama White House. Of course, substantial Democratic majorities created opportunities for policy changes; but apparent openings to pass new legislation were compromised by significant intraparty divisions, which would make it hard to overcome GOP opposition reinforced by filibusters in the Senate. In the 111th Congress, as always, the ranks of congressional Democrats included not only liberals but also moderates and conservatives who oppose tightening government regulations or raising taxes even on the very wealthy. On key issues, ideological splits were reinforced by regional divisions. For example, Obama's call for energy reform was haunted by the split between Democratic lawmakers from coal-producing states and those from regions with businesses focused on developing other sources of energy; and health care reform was slowed, in part, because of tensions between legislators from the (mostly midwestern) states that provide health care at lower cost and the (eastern and western) states where costs are higher (even taking account of the overall cost of living). Immigration is yet another topic that splits legislators within each party along largely regional lines, including the Democrats.

Notwithstanding such typical sources of push and pull in U.S. politics, Obama's push for changes in federal policies started out strong. The new president enjoyed sky-high public approval ratings and quickly persuaded Congress to pass the American Recovery and Reinvestment Act (the so-called stimulus), which injected nearly a trillion dollars into the economy and included initial resources for new policy initiatives in education, clean energy production, and health care.[14] Congressional Democrats passed and Obama quickly signed legislation about fair pay and children's health insurance that had been vetoed under President George W. Bush.

Somewhat to the surprise of D.C. insiders (who expect new presidents to pivot away from electoral rhetoric), President Obama pressed forward to meet the promises he made during the 2008 campaign. His first budget was called *A New Era of Responsibility: Renewing America's Promise,* and was far from the usual snoozy bureaucratic treatise. In visionary language, the budget called for regulatory shifts and new directions in taxing and spending. It spelled out proposals to move away from providing federal subsidies to favored private industries and tax cuts for the very wealthy, while shifting resources toward broadening access to higher education, stimulating K–12 school reform, paying for health insurance for all Americans, and encouraging new environmentally friendly practices. In contrast to the Republican legislative strategy of relentlessly cutting taxes and talking about spending cuts without delivering them, Obama candidly proposed a fiscal policy that would expand social benefits for middle- and lower-income Americans and pay for them with specific spending cuts and tax increases on the privileged. Following this blueprint, Obama soon urged Congress to work on bold legislation for comprehensive health reform, on a new national energy policy, and on tightened regulation of Wall Street practices. In other key domestic policy areas such as labor law reform and immigration reform, his administration realized the futility of calling for quick congressional action— Democrats were divided, Republicans were uncooperative, and the votes were not there. But Obama's administration nevertheless took immediate steps to further significant changes through the federal bureaucracy and regulatory agencies.[15]

Although energetic, the Obama administration's efforts were soon slowed and obstructed by more than garden-variety ambivalences in public opinion and divisions among Democrats. Extraordinary partisan obstruction and intense political blowback greeted Obama undertakings from the get-go. My analysis of how and why this happened in 2009 and 2010 necessarily goes beyond the usual timeless political science narrative to highlight critical macroscopic aspects of institutions, unfolding historical trends, and coincidences of timing—all of which account for obstacles and magnified political opposition to even the most cautious Obama initiatives. To bring the big picture into view, I draw contrasts between the launch of the first New Deal of the 1930s and the early efforts of Obama's change-oriented presidency.

This comparison across time does not presume that Obama's early presidency is similar to the original New Deal. On the contrary, I use comparisons across eras to *highlight contrasts* between two periods of reformist Democratic politics amid deep economic crises. In the pages to come, I will compare the shape and timing of the economic crises of the early 1930s and 2008 to 2010; delineate the influence of long-festering realignments of ideology and partisanship; and compare the structure and effects of media institutions that have influence possibilities for authoritative presidential communication in different eras of U.S politics. Above all, I will highlight the crucial difference between launching *new* peacetime federal interventions, as FDR did in the first New Deal, and Obama's efforts to revise and redirect already-entrenched federal programs and practices. Comparisons across historical periods highlight major shifts in institutions and clarify different flashpoints of conflict and sequences of change. They help us outline the changing shape of the forest in U.S. politics, and stay away from the obsession with particular trees, or leaves on trees, that typifies most scholarship and pundit commentary.

REFORMIST PRESIDENTS CONFRONT
ECONOMIC MELTDOWNS

It's the nature of the economic crisis, stupid. That is the place to start for understanding why managing a national economic emergency does not necessarily reinforce reformist policy undertakings or reward them politically. Although Franklin Delano Roosevelt and Barack Obama both came into office as change-oriented Democrats, the timing, nature, and severity of the economic crises each faced explain crucial differences between Obama's debut in 2009–2010 and FDR's launch of the New Deal during 1933–1934. Roosevelt took office several years into the Great Depression, when the U.S. economy was at a nadir; with some 25 percent of Americans unemployed, the nation was begging for strong federal action. Congressional Republicans and Democrats alike were ready to vote for the bills FDR sent them, sometimes without even having fully written texts of bills before Congress voted.[16] American citizens battered by the Great Depression were open to the direct federal creation of jobs. By contrast, Obama took office amid a sudden financial seizure that was just beginning to push the national economy into a downturn of as-yet-undetermined proportions. Obama would end up being associated with steep economic decline and severe job losses, as Republican president Herbert Hoover once was. In addition, since the American people as of early 2009 had yet to experience much of what was to come in the Great

Recession, they could not know what to demand or expect from initial federal recovery efforts. Obama started off without FDR's clear-cut opening to dramatize a full-blown national economic emergency and pursue a full range of policies, including direct federal creation of large numbers of jobs. This was to prove ominously fateful for his presidency.

The nature as well as phasing of the financially induced crisis starting in 2008 affected Obama's economic leadership, real and perceived. Obama's electoral triumph over McCain gained momentum during the Wall Street meltdown that became apparent in September 2008, as conventional wisdom has long recognized. But looking deeper, we can see that candidate Obama was drawn into cooperation with the outgoing Bush administration starting well before the November election, as well as during the presidential transition. Decades earlier, FDR had deliberately avoided invitations to work together from outgoing Republican president Herbert Hoover. But in 2008, with the economic meltdown just getting started, Obama could not avoid transitional efforts to prevent the initial Wall Street crisis from spiraling out of control, a catastrophe that would have taken down the world financial system and plunged the United States into a massive and prolonged depression. FDR came into office when the patient was near death, while Obama wanted to keep the patient's raging fever from turning into pneumonia. In consequence, just as he was winning the 2008 election and preparing to move into the White House, Obama seemed to be holding hands with the modern-day equivalent of Herbert Hoover, discredited outgoing GOP president George W. Bush.

Cooperation to deal with Wall Street woes started in earnest during the 2008 presidential campaign in mid-September, when GOP candidate McCain tried to call off the first presidential debate and hold a summit at the Bush White House. As Jonathan Alter reminds us in *The Promise: President Obama, Year One,* this campaign stunt backfired on McCain because Obama was the one who looked cool, calm, wise, and in charge.[17] Another aspect of this episode mattered just as much, if not more. Soon-to-be president-elect Obama became engaged with Bush administration efforts to mitigate the financial crisis through the politically unpopular decision to build congressional support for a massive financial rescue plan, the Troubled Asset Relief Program (TARP). Starting at that misguided September 2008 session at the White House, Obama gained confidence that he could master complex issues and work with financial experts. Ironically, the insurgent Democratic candidate who campaigned by promising a bottom-up approach to economic growth and renewal in America started his "presidential" economic efforts amid a bipartisan scramble to help Wall Street first. A couple of months later, President-elect Obama would also urge outgoing President Bush to support legislation to rescue collapsing U.S. auto companies. No incoming Democratic president could stand by while key industries headquartered in the Midwest went down the tubes, but, again, this looked to many Americans outside the Midwest like a selective taxpayer bailout. To millions of Americans beginning to face the realities of declining family fortunes, underwater mortgages, and looming pink slips, TARP and the auto rescues alike looked like helping the big guys float free while ordinary Americans were left to drown.

Obama's initial economic efforts may also have limited his purview going forward. After his election, the president-elect quickly decided that two Wall Street–connected experts,

Timothy Geithner and Lawrence Summers, would lead his White House economic advisory team.[18] In a financially induced crisis, Obama believed they were uniquely qualified to figure out where reforms were needed—and perhaps persuade bankers to help the larger economy going forward. But building this kind of economic team also meant that Obama was not going to hear day-to-day from other kinds of economic experts who thought of job creation as the first-order challenge, or who saw U.S. economic recovery over the longer term as requiring commitments to structural transformation and seeding innovative new industries. Drawing on established macroeconomic wisdom and the "common sense" of the financial community to which they are connected, Summers and Geithner advised Obama to counter the Wall Street crisis with bank bailouts that imposed minimal penalties, hoping to cajole and soothe bankers into resuming lending. They urged Obama to avoid nationalizing banks and forgo other aggressive steps out of fear that such undertakings could cause "a disastrous run on those banks."[19] Beyond that, Obama's team, joined by other orthodox economic advisors, urged spending a lot of federal money as quickly as possible—which necessarily meant spending on established programs that could be expanded without new planning or protracted negotiations. Investments in infrastructure and green jobs, for example, were set aside as requiring too much planning or risking protracted litigation. Tax cuts would also be added into the Recovery Act, accounting for a third of the overall stimulus package. Calm the bankers, cut taxes, and quickly spend as much as Congress would enact for projects that could be implemented without a lot of corruption or litigation, and then be patient as the economy slowly recovered over the course of 2010 and 2011: that was the prescription.

Some outside economists like Paul Krugman urged the Obama White House to push for more than a trillion-dollar stimulus and keep the proportion devoted to tax cuts to a minimum.[20] But such advice did not seem realistic to the fledgling Obama White House, which felt it had to stay under a trillion to win congressional support. Perhaps naïvely, Obama also tried to woo congressional Republicans with substantial up-front tax cuts of the sorts they had claimed to support in the past. His outreached hand was slapped down, as Obama got fewer than a handful of GOP votes in return for his gestures. A year and a half later, once it became clear that growth still lagged into 2010, expert postmortems focused on the use of taxes instead of more stimulative direct spending in the American Recovery and Reinvestment Act and bemoaned the insufficient size of the stimulus package. But President Obama's early choices were understandable for a brand-new president who was trying to induce recovery in a highly financialized national economy and who had just promised the electorate he would change the political tone in Washington. As for the size of the stimulus itself, it is not clear that any larger package could have gotten through Congress.

In retrospect, the fact that Obama's economic recovery strategy was not truly a jobs program—or proclaimed as such to the watching public—mattered more than the sheer size of the effort.[21] The American Recovery and Reinvestment Act is better understood as a Hail Mary pass to goose aggregate economic growth by 2010, hoping that jobs would come back in tandem with the revival of overall GDP growth (or following soon after growth resumed). The absence of a "jobs program" stemmed, in part, from the decision of Democratic leaders to push the large stimulus package through Congress very soon after Obama's inauguration, both to stave off the looming financial and economic disaster as best they could and to conserve time within the president's honeymoon period for the pursuit of long-planned efforts such as comprehensive health care reform. The idea was to get some of those reforms through in ample time to take effect before the next elections. Yet this approach meant that the White House largely deferred to congressional appropriators, letting them push money into their long-standing wish lists. A bold plan for creating new jobs would have taken much longer to formulate, and would have run into many congressional buzz saws.

There were downsides and future political bills to be paid, however. President Obama's quickly devised economic recovery strategy confused American citizens, many of whom did not see how heightened federal spending, funded through a growing deficit, could work. Most citizens wanted jobs saved or made immediately available, but Obama's bailouts, spending, and tax cuts would, at best, bring about only a gradual recovery with jobs appearing last, after banks and businesses recovered. By the summer of 2010, even aggregate growth was slowing, and unemployment remained above 9 percent (a pattern that repeated itself again in 2011). Understandably, Americans believed that Obama—supported by his Democratic Congress—had first "saved" Wall Street and other corporate giants, and had left much of Main Street foundering. During the run-in to the November 2010 election, and afterward into 2011, Obama and his party were hampered by too little job growth and the sense among many

Americans that "federal spending does not work" to create economic recovery—or, worse, that the usual insiders are the real beneficiaries of recovery efforts.[22] Obama's administration reinforced this narrative by privileging deficit reduction as a key goal, starting in 2010—but the underlying difficulty was always that his administration did not come to be associated with sufficient job growth. In one of several piercing ironies, the winds of populism and change that swept Obama into office in 2008 turned against him two years later, and threatened to block further government actions to promote economic recovery, spur job creation, and broaden social opportunity.

REPUBLICAN OBSTRUCTION

At the start of the first New Deal, President Franklin Roosevelt enjoyed bipartisan support for recovery efforts launched at an economic nadir. Decades later, candidate Obama partnered with Republican officials to handle the financial crisis during the closing days of the Bush presidency, yet his own initial recovery proposal got virtually no votes from congressional Republicans in early 2009, even as their home states clamored for emergency fiscal relief. As the months went by, Republican opposition hardened, as grassroots activists and ideological opponents of government reinforced GOP refusal to work with Obama.

The nation was facing a true national economic emergency in late 2008 and 2009, so why did Republican Party leaders in the 111th Congress refuse to cooperate with a popular new president? (They refused from the start, well before the Tea Party gathered force.) This question has special poignancy given the obvious falsehood of charges that Obama was "antibusiness" or hostile to free enterprise. As we have seen,

Obama appointed Wall Street–friendly advisors and worked continuously to shore up banks and revive business activity. In tandem with the outgoing Bush administration, the nascent Obama White House tried to prop up and revive the private sector in the U.S. economy. During 2009 and 2010, corporate balance sheets recovered long before the fortunes of workers, families, and small businesses in most of mainstream America.

Analysts in social science often treat politics as a mere reflection of economic or class interests. But the key to the GOP turn toward hard-line opposition lies in political forces and strategy, not business concerns. Following the 2008 election, Republican congressional ranks were sharply depleted, and party leaders inside and outside government were attuned to a dispirited, heavily older and white voter base centered in the South and parts of the West and Midwest. The loudest voices in the GOP firmament, moreover, were flamboyant right-wing media commentators at Fox News and in the right-wing blogosphere, commentators without governing responsibilities who could freely respond to—and stoke— the most intense popular fears and angers in the conservative GOP base. Whipping up fears and controversies, in fact, maximizes profits in the entertainment and propaganda industry. GOP officeholders and would-be candidates were quickly affected. With a lot of their voting base at a boil and likely to stay that way, GOP leaders in office saw little advantage in crossing swords with rabble-rousing pundits or trying to dampen voter enthusiasm to turn out next time. Nor did GOP leaders see any advantage in working with Obama. If cooperation produced popular legislation or spurred economic recovery, Republicans assumed that Obama would get the credit—so why help him? Adding up all the political pluses and minuses, GOP congressional leaders decided from the start of Obama's presidency to pursue a strategy of all-out opposition—a strategy they could hope to implement, given that smaller, more conservative congressional flocks were easier to manage. Congressional GOPers tend to wander off the reservation less readily than Democrats anyway, and the results of the 2008 election left a more right-wing set of cats for House Minority Leader John Boehner and Senate Minority Leader Mitch McConnell to herd.

All-out opposition to Obama and Democratic initiatives was a cold-blooded political bet made possible because the Great Recession was just starting on the heels of the Wall Street bailout undertaken by the outgoing Bush administration. Two-thirds of House Republicans had voted against the unpopular bailout when it first came up under Bush, and only half voted for the final bailout legislation, despite pleas from Bush officials and business leaders after the stock market plunged following the abortive first congressional vote. As the Democrats took charge, congressional Republicans aimed to pin the unpopular bailout on Obama; indeed, they succeeded in convincing many voters that the bailout and the American Recovery and Reinvestment Act (the stimulus) were one and the same. It was all a bunch of expensive federal handouts, congressional Republicans told the public. That message gained a lot of traction, even if particular GOP representatives and senators regularly went home for ribbon-cutting ceremonies celebrating job-creating stimulus projects they had voted against in Washington. Republicans held the ceremonies while decrying the programs because they knew that Americans like the specifics of government spending, even when the public worries about higher spending and possible future taxes overall. Republican strategists also knew that if unemployment reached a high level and remained elevated, unified Republican opposition to Obama's agenda in Washington could position their party in the next elections as the only alternative to what they would be able to label a "failed" Democratic Congress and presidency. Why help President Obama and congressional Democrats spur robust economic growth or federal powers to create large numbers of jobs any time before November 2010 or November 2012?

In addition to facing partisan efforts to slow-pedal economic growth and blame him for using emergency federal spending to stave off dire economic troubles that originated during the Bush presidency, President Obama inherited a huge federal budget deficit from the Bush era—bills run up by off-budget wars, tax cuts for the very wealthy, and a new Medicare drug benefit not paid for with future revenue streams.[23] Add the inherited unpaid bills and declining taxes due to the recession to the unavoidable cost of bailouts and the stimulus, and it was easy to see that President Obama started out with deficit problems that would only grow—quite apart from funding for any of the new long-term reform measures Obama had promised the electorate during 2008. Republicans knew they could take political advantage of the new president's terrible luck in the coincidence of a downspiraling economic crisis with his early legislative efforts to fashion a second New Deal, and they decided to do so.

PARTISAN AND IDEOLOGICAL POLARIZATION

Because of the very early crystallization of GOP opposition, rightward ideological polarization expressed through party politics grew steadily more intense during Obama's first years in office. Barack Obama's presidential campaign had given voice to widespread public desires for bipartisan cooperation; and President Obama repeatedly reached out to Republicans in Washington and beyond. All to no avail. Bipartisan hopes never became more than whispers into gale-force winds.

We need to keep in mind the longer-term trends that Obama was powerless to counter, especially once his GOP opponents chose unified obstruction. Decades ago, during the middle of the twentieth century, ideological and party divisions did not entirely overlap in U.S. electoral politics. During and after the first New Deal, there were many conservative southern Democrats and a fair number of moderate to slightly liberal northern Republicans. Congress often functioned through "old boy" bipartisan deals. Old-fashioned interparty deals started to disappear after the civil rights revolution of the 1960s, as the Republican Party turned toward the right and became the home of white southerners. Polarization proceeded during the last part of the twentieth century, especially at the level of elected representatives and advocacy elites. Ideological conservatives gravitated toward the Republican Party and liberals gained ground in the Democratic Party.[24] Beyond such sorting, conservative activists used money and grassroots campaigns to pull the Republican Party even further to the right, especially in congressional and public debates over social issues and taxes.[25] Ideological homogenization and polarization have gone further on the Republican than on the Democratic side, and polarized congressional voting has tended to facilitate conservative obstruction of social policy initiatives to help lower- or middle-income people.[26]

No wonder, then, that when a new Democratic president arrived in office in 2009 promising to use federal initiatives actively to favor lower- and middle-income people, long-operating conservative forces were determined to mount all the opposition they could. Their efforts were enabled by procedural rules and customs in Congress that allow minorities to delay or obstruct majority decision-making. During much of the 111th Congress, the Democrats had substantial margins in both the House and Senate, but only in the former were they truly "in control" (if and when they could get their intraparty act together). The Speaker of the House can use simple majority votes to control which bills come to a vote, when the vote occurs, and the handling of amendments. Senate rules, by contrast, create myriad possibilities for slowing things down.[27] During the 111th Congress, a single senator could object and prevent majority action by placing a "hold" on nominations and bills. By Senate custom, a minority can request many delays in committees and on the floor— and a minority of forty-one senators can filibuster, demanding a supermajority vote on virtually any matter. The need for sixty votes to break delaying tactics of the filibuster used to arise only occasionally, when truly major issues were at stake. But in recent decades, the filibuster has been invoked with increasing frequency, turning from an extraordinary expression into a routine obstructive tactic.[28] Under Barack Obama, Republican obstructionists decided to invoke the supermajority rule on almost every issue small and large. In a radical departure from past practices, Republican obstructionists have prevented President Obama from assembling his administration in normal time, forestalled much-needed judicial appointments to fill accumulating court vacancies, and blocked most reform initiatives. Remarkably, the filibuster was invoked more often during 2009 than during the entire decade of the 1950s.[29]

The press emphasized that Obama and the Democrats held a supposedly "filibuster-proof" sixty-vote majority for many months during the 111th Congress—from the time when Senator Al Franken was seated in July 2009 following Minnesota's contested election until mid-January 2010, when a Republican, Scott Brown, surprisingly won a special election to fill the seat of deceased senator Ted Kennedy. But in truth, there never was a reliable sixty-vote margin. Independent senator Joseph Lieberman could never be counted upon to stick with anyone's team (or even stick with his own previous positions), and various conservative Democrats regularly defected. Obama's Democratic margins in Congress never reached the level enjoyed by previous Democratic presidents.[30] Throughout his presidential term, Jimmy Carter had a stronger Senate majority than Obama. And FDR, John Kennedy, and Lyndon Johnson had larger majorities to work with when they pushed far-reaching social programs—although back then, of course, many Democrats were southern conservatives. The record shows that early twenty-first-century Republicans have been unwilling to allow an elected Democratic president of the United States to govern amid a major national emergency.

Because Republicans in the 111th Congress remained almost entirely opposed to Obama's initiatives, the drama in one policy area after another focused on what sorts of Democratic coalitions could be formed, and whether a few defections on any given issue would make forward movement impossible. Obviously, legislative action was ever-precarious in the Senate, where any one or two Democrats could kill all possibility of forward movement (unless an equal number plus one Republican votes could be found). But even in the 111th House, where the Democrats had a seventy-five-vote margin in a majoritarian chamber, various kinds of issues could peel off dozens of Democrats. That happened when ideological or regional concerns were aroused—for example, among coal-state Democrats opposed to environmental measures—or when businesses connected to particular representatives started pushing back against Democratic proposals.

Back in the original New Deal of the 1930s, congressional coalitions were often decisive and dispositive as well. President Roosevelt may have enjoyed bipartisan support in the opening months of his first term, but a "conservative coalition" formed in Congress by 1934 and placed limits on his initiatives for the remainder of the domestic New Deal.[31] Even so, New Deal divisions were not a purely partisan matter because many of the conservatives were southern Democrats—indeed they were Democratic chairs of powerful congressional committees. During the 1930s, as now, proposed federal reforms evoked fierce counterpressures. But the divisions and counterpressures facing Obama have been both partisan and ideological, indeed an overlapping and dysfunctional mélange of both at the same time.

The use of GOP filibusters to mire the Senate in repeated delays ensured that Americans saw a dysfunctional government, with everything slowed to a crawl during the critical early months of Obama's change-oriented presidency. Instead of seeming authoritatively in control during the 111th Congress, Obama's White House repeatedly had to caucus with Democratic House Speaker Nancy Pelosi and Democratic Senate majority leader Harry Reid, looking for ways to coordinate agendas and move key bills through the many hurdles in the legislative process, especially in the Senate. Obama and his White House aides knew that the 111th Congress was their best chance to further big legislative reforms. To take advantage of congressional Democratic majorities, they devoted enormous amounts of time to working with the Democratic congressional leaders to assemble fragile and shifting coalitions. The watching public, however, did not necessarily understand why Democrats spent so much time negotiating among themselves, or why the president could not just tell a Democratic Congress to "get it done." Democratic maneuvers seemed highly partisan—because Republicans sat them out and sniped from the sidelines. White House efforts to work with Democratic leaders looked very "liberal" as well because liberal versus conservative differences have become so closely aligned with the major party labels.

The alignment of ideology and party mattered in another way. Much of our national system of political communication is geared toward giving extra voice to criticisms from the minority party. In the Obama administration, therefore, Republicans enjoyed the regular access to the media that the minority party automatically receives—and they could denounce Democratic efforts as ultra-"liberal" even when those efforts were fairly moderate. GOP leaders also used their media access to cry foul about the very congressional consultations they themselves boycotted and tried to obstruct. On the one hand, GOP leaders refused to enter into legislative bargains or talk about compromises with the White House; on the other hand, they claimed that Democrats were excluding them in favor of high-handed partisan fiat! Republicans were able to prevent Democratic action, or else force

Democrats into elaborate bargaining to hold coalitions together—all the while decrying partisanship and blaming Democrats for delays and special deals (such as the "Cornhusker Kickback" used during the Senate endgame in health reform to cajole Ben Nelson of Nebraska to join other Democrats to break the Republican filibuster in late 2009). It was a neat trick, open only to an obstructionist congressional minority operating without responsibility for governing in a highly polarized polity.

Through all of this, Obama and Democrats of the 111th Congress ended up looking to the larger public both responsible for partisan rancor and incompetent at settling legislative quarrels. Yet the real culprits were institutional rules that fostered deadlocks, plus the ideologically aligned ultrapartisanship now bedeviling U.S. politics. Obama and his congressional allies had to absorb the public disapproval and loss of time associated with assembling complex coalitions in the face of GOP obstruction. There was little choice, if the president and his allies wanted to act to try to revive the economy and accomplish reforms promised during the 2008 campaigns. Enduring repeated Republican charges decrying "partisanship" and "deal making" was the price for trying to govern in an era where ideology and party align so closely. The political bill would come due for Democrats in future elections.

FRAGMENTED MEDIA AND THE LIMITS OF AUTHORITATIVE COMMUNICATION

Decades ago, President Franklin Delano Roosevelt enjoyed a comparatively unfiltered opportunity to communicate with much of the American citizenry. Although major newspapers were largely hostile to Roosevelt during the 1930s, his famous fireside chats broadcast on the radio reached into millions of homes, revealing both the scope of that broadly shared communication modality and the eagerness of all Americans to hear directly from their president in a time of national crisis.[32] The media dynamics surrounding Obama's presidency have been quite different. White House and Democratic messages are filtered and garbled by commentators, while conservatives determined to attack Obama and his party have plentiful opportunities to broadcast their attacks. At the same time, direct popular mobilization waned among Democrats after their party took charge in the nation's capital.

During the 2007 and 2008 primary and general election campaigns, Barack Obama and the Democratic Party proved extraordinarily adept at shaping public perceptions and using a mesh of old and new media to motivate and activate voters.[33] Observers assumed that Obama as president would continue to frame public issues in major speeches; and they presumed that the Obama White House and Democratic National Committee would continue to communicate with and engage millions of supporters, not just to further the president's policy agenda and ensure his eventual reelection, but also to support congressional Democrats who did the heavy lifting to further the presidential agenda. It did not work out that way during Obama's first two years in office, and we need to explore why.

Part of the explanation for weak liberal citizen engagement after Obama took office lies in the reorganization of Obama for America (the grassroots election operation that mobilized supporters during the 2008 election) into an arm of the Democratic National Committee called Organizing for America. This reorganization in effect subjected local and grassroots networks to attempted direction from above, with Organizing for America honchos trying to cheerlead for whatever the White House wanted at any given moment during complex legislative maneuvers in 2009 and 2010. Alas for them, grassroots activism works better when it is relatively spontaneous and at most loosely linked to official institutions. In addition, citizens are much more readily mobilized for a high-stakes presidential contest on a date certain than they are during a congressionally centered year-long battle like the fifteen-month campaign for health care reform legislation during 2009 and 2010.[34] In the health care reform battle and other congressional imbroglios, President Obama rarely took strong stands on policy specifics, preferring to let legislators hash out enactable bills. But this meant that Organizing for America and other would-be grassroots organizers at the edges of the Democratic Party could not even tell people exactly what they were fighting for, let alone when or whether it would come to a critical juncture of decision.

The mystery about Obama's first two years of presidential messaging seems deeper, however, and cracking this mystery leads us to look at the structure and dynamics of the public communications media. To be sure, Barack Obama on the national stage has always been a "new media user." Just as FDR used radio fireside chats to get very regularly into the ears of ordinary Americans, Obama's presidential campaign was creative in the use of Internet and social media communications, and President Obama records weekly YouTube presidential addresses that are watched by millions of Americans at the click of a computer mouse. Obama is also effective in sit-down interviews with journalists, supplemented by appearances on "soft"-format popular television shows such as *The View* and late-night comedy hours, in order to reach people without going through formal news conferences or other formats filtered by professional reporters.

But here the cross-era similarities in creative presidential communication end because Obama's White House faces an institutionally fragmented media environment that segments listening, viewing, and Internet-using audiences in ways that make attention fleeting and divide Americans into segmented communicative and reality communities.[35] In the early decades of television, Americans tended to be stuck with the same three major networks presenting homogenized news broadcasts at dinnertime. But those days are long gone, now that we have proliferating cable television channels and many kinds of additional media. Many Americans find it easy to escape news pretty much altogether, watching entertainment or sports instead. And among those who do follow political news, interpretive subcommunities proliferate. Older, white conservatives watch and listen to very different news outlets from younger, diverse, independent, and liberal Americans.[36] All contemporary institutional leaders, including the president of the United States, find it hard to get an overall message through to most Americans at the same time—a situation that is somewhat modified during presidential elections and huge crises like 9/11, but otherwise prevails.

Beyond that, twenty-first-century Democrats have to contend with a rightward-skewed media landscape. Fox News, right-wing talk radio, and various conservative bloggers are openly partisan, disseminating interpretations that are not only openly right-wing but often also not based on fact. Interconnected conservative outlets give huge agenda-setting opportunities to right-wing controversy-mongers like Andrew Breitbart because they echo and spread extreme charges that put Democrats on the defensive. Issue entrepreneurs pushing controversies from the margins can quickly inject a fake or overblown problem into intense coverage across channels.[37]

Fox and other conservative media outlets do not have a monopoly, of course. But, ironically, "mainstream" media outlets trying to compete for viewers and listeners on tight budgets can end up following agendas set from the right. Other networks try to compete with Fox either through imitation of formats if not content (CNN, quite often) or through a degree of differentiation (MSNBC); either way, the premium is placed on magnifying or arguing with highly provocative voices that first appear on Fox (or on right-wing blogs en route to Fox). In due course, even the proudest old-line media, including newspapers like the *New York Times,* allow some of their agenda to be taken up by topics launched from the right-wing noise and echo machine. With only shallow efforts at fact checking, nonconservative outlets pick up colorful accusations, take polls about them, and sponsor endless debates among talking heads. Topics that matter very little, even entirely fake controversies, get sustained coverage— which suggests to casual viewers or listeners that they are real problems. Meanwhile, true national dilemmas are not discussed. Public discourse gets overwhelmed with trivia and lies—crowding out attention to real problems or concerted efforts to tackle intractable national challenges.

In sum, because today's U.S. media system involves the coexistence of frankly right-wing outlets with other, commercially straightened outlets scrambling to attract audiences, old-fashioned journalistic practices such as fact checking and attempts to present in-depth, balanced news have gone out the window. For a reformist Democratic president trying to cope with huge national challenges, this media environment is toxic. While Republican attack messages are delivered intact regardless of any factual basis, presidential and Democratic messages are garbled. And amid all of the cacophony going on 24/7 all year long, it is very difficult for the U.S. president (let alone congressional leaders trying to push forward with difficult legislative initiatives) to communicate accurate information about what is going on. Citizens end up either riled up or confused, or both.

Acknowledging these facts about current media institutions and dynamics in the early twenty-first-century United States, many critics have nevertheless questioned the communications strategy of the Obama White House during Obama's first years in office, especially on economic issues. In one of his priority areas, health care reform, Obama gave major speeches and orchestrated theatrically effective issue forums at key intervals during 2009 and early 2010, displaying presidential leadership and offering framings that proved influential beyond as well as within the Beltway. U.S. policies in Iraq and Afghanistan have also been repeatedly addressed by the president in nationally visible settings. But from 2009 on, President Obama was curiously reticent about the nation's economic crisis and what he was doing to address it. During his honeymoon period in the first half of 2009, President Obama did not engage in sustained and nationally televised public explanations about the reasons the stimulus was structured as it was, how it differed from the Bush Wall Street bailouts, and why government spending can function to create millions of jobs. Later, he said much more about the federal budget deficit than about the issues of economic growth and job creation that really concerned most Americans. Although Obama traveled the country highlighting economic initiatives and progress in selected areas, such efforts lacked the galvanizing, agenda-setting effect of a major speech or sustained national communications strategy; and their fragmented focus inherently restricted the White House's ability to present a coherent economic plan. Not until *after* the Democrats sustained massive losses in the House in late 2010, not until after the GOP gained strength in early 2011, did President Obama finally offer a compelling vision for the future of the U.S. economy, starting in his State of the Union address delivered on January 25, 2011, and resuming later in 2011 when the president pivoted away from discussions of budget cutting to champion the American Jobs Act. The positive public response in both instances suggests that he should have tried a stronger focus on jobs much earlier. For too many months, especially in the spring and summer of 2011, Obama's administration appeared mired in backroom negotiations over how to slash spending in the federal budget—an approach certain to worry the public and retard rather than accelerate economic growth and job creation.

Perhaps Obama and his original economic advisors believed an overall framing of economic strategy in socially understandable and value-laden terms was too difficult to pull off or was unnecessary—a common mistake for Democratic policy wonks who presume that facts "speak for themselves" and that sharply pitched communications are inappropriate. If so, President Obama and his White House advisors failed to understand that American citizens have heard for many years a steady stream of arguments about how government spending hurts the economy and tax cuts are the only way to spur growth and create jobs.[38] Conservatives do all they can to keep this narrative alive, to the detriment of Democrats who want to use government actively to spur economic growth and buffer vulnerable families during economic downturns. Given that prior backdrop of public beliefs and misunderstandings, a Democratic president circa 2010 needed to invest time and institutional resources to effectively frame a bold economic recovery strategy, if he wanted citizens to understand why he proposed what he did—especially if he wanted citizens to be able to track successes and shortfalls and remain patient through a protracted recovery process.

Whatever the structure of media institutions or the dynamics of partisan messaging, the president always has the possibility of using the bully pulpit to communicate nationally. As FDR proved back in the 1930s, and as Ronald Reagan demonstrated again—when he struggled to preserve presidential power amid an economic downturn in the 1980s—citizens in a democracy need and want a sense of strategic presidential leadership in a period of crisis. Whether or not Larry Summers thought a given measure would pass Ivy League muster, whether or not Rahm Emanuel thought it would get through Congress, President Obama needed from early 2009 onward to convey to Americans his signature plans for national economic recovery and job creation. Most citizens would probably have accepted setbacks and delays with some patience, if they felt sure that the president was leading us to a better place. Obama's failure to engage more consistently in high-profile public leadership on the economy constitutes, in an important sense, democratic political malpractice. For much of his first term, Obama botched a central function of the presidency in a period of economic crisis—and if he is not reelected to a second term, his early shortfall in this vital area of democratic communication will be a significant part of the explanation.

CREATING VERSUS RESHAPING NATIONAL POLICIES

Finally, we come to the biggest difference between the 1930s and now—the contrast that best explains the political blow-back that greeted Obama's efforts to further reforms in health care, higher education, energy and the environment, and federal taxation. Back in the 1930s, the New Dealers in Congress and in the FDR administration were advocating *new kinds* of federal government interventions—new financial regulations, unprecedented national policies like minimum wage and maximum hour rules, Social Security, unemployment insurance, and new rights for labor unions to organize. Previously, apart from setting tariffs, helping farmers, and seeding infrastructure and western expansion, the U.S. federal government had intervened actively in economic and social affairs only temporarily during major wars. The New Dealers, amid a massive Great Depression, were advocating a series of innovative permanent peacetime interventions into the mature industrial economy. They were selling governmental reforms amid a huge economic emergency—and, ultimately, World War II reinforced and helped entrench much of what they started during the Depression itself.

Today, by contrast, Obama and his Democratic allies offer not first-time interventions but revised frameworks for already pervasive federal regulations, benefits, and taxes. Obama arrived in office following a half-century of previous accretions of pervasive regulatory and fiscal interventions—

and set out to reverse some and redirect others. What is more, the new president and his allies came to office dogged by already-ballooning federal deficits. Finding new resources for redistributive social benefits—such as more generous college loans for low-income families, or subsidies to help poor and lower-middle-income people afford health insurance—required that Obama and his congressional supporters raise new revenues or recapture funds previously devoted to other federal programs. These twenty-first-century New Dealers launched legislative and regulatory overhauls just as an economic freefall was gathering steam, not at its nadir. And in contrast to the positive impact of World War II on many New Deal initiatives, the wars Obama inherited in Afghanistan and Iraq drained rather than reinforced economic recovery and diverted attention from domestic reforms.

Turn on the television just about any day, or pick up a newspaper, and you will hear media pundits, even the occasional academic, proclaiming that Americans in the early twenty-first century are fighting about "government" versus "the free market." This is nonsense. Over the past six decades, D.C. Democrats *and* Republicans alike have presided over more or less steady hikes in taxes and tax subsidies, plus expansion of regulation and defense and social spending, with much of the growth financed by increasing deficits because politicians of both parties have been eager to hand out business subsidies and finance wars while cutting taxes—to the point that the United States is the least taxed among advanced capitalist economies with ever-reduced tax claims on the exploding wealth of millionaires and billionaires.[39] Both parties have participated in building up a massive, ramified, expensive, and pervasive national state that actively deploys subsidies, tax breaks, and regulations to shape the economy and redistribute wealth, security, and opportunity.[40] On the margin, Democrats tilt the tax advantages and subsidies toward working families and the middle class, while Republicans since 1980 have pushed subsidies and advantages toward favored industries while slashing taxes for the very wealthy.[41] But prior to 2011, neither party cut back in any important respect. Consequently, every region of the United States, and every industry and social stratum, has had a steadily growing stake in existing federal interventions into the economy and the society.

The upshot of the situation just described is that when a change-oriented president like Obama arrives in Washington aiming to transform the patterns and distributive impact of federal government interventions, he is not starting from scratch like FDR. He is redirecting resources—and at the same time asking some citizens and interests already enjoying regulatory advantages, governmental subsidies or benefits, and tax breaks to accept less. Social science tells us that those asked to give up something are quite alert to their potential disadvantage and quick to mobilize against change, while those who might benefit from rearrangements in some hypothetical future are likely to be skeptical, and certainly not yet concretely accustomed to the new advantages they might enjoy. Potential beneficiaries remain mostly disengaged—and in an era when government is distrusted, they may be wary and skeptical. The disparity of mobilization becomes worse when the previously advantaged are wealthier or better organized, or both, while the potential beneficiaries are lower- or lower-middle-income Americans who may not vote regularly and have not been previously mobilized by groups advocating their interests. Across strata, the elderly enjoy some degree of leverage, to the degree that the AARP steps in to lobby government and to keep seniors informed about legislation that affects Social Security and Medicare.[42] But no comparable lobbying allies exist for non-elderly less-privileged Americans. Add to the organizational imbalances the demonstrated finding that officeholders pay more heed to the preferences of the rich than to those of middle-class or poor citizens, and the dilemma of how to leverage equality-enhancing changes in public policy becomes all the more acute.[43]

Indeed, Obama's attempt to create a new New Deal has been bedeviled by the knotty dilemma of how to shift policies in redistributive directions, in ways that cut against current political inequalities. Health insurance coverage for lower- and middle-income uninsured Americans could be financed only through hard-fought steps to place new charges on businesses and the well-to-do.[44] Enhanced Pell grants for lower-income college students and better loan terms for middle-class college students required a battle with private bankers accustomed to receiving guaranteed profits for administering federally backed loans without risk.[45] Proposals for new energy policies aroused strong (and ultimately decisive) resistance from coal and oil and gas interests, including businesses with a strong presence in regions represented by congressional Democrats.[46]

What is more, as we see in ongoing tax and budget battles fought at fever pitch, Obama's 2008 campaign promise to allow the expiration of George W. Bush's tax breaks for the very highest income earners faced fierce pushback and was undermined by Democratic skittishness, even when the president's party enjoyed congressional majorities in 2009 and 2010.[47] After Republicans took over the House in the 112th Congress, they put in place rules that favor additional tax cuts.

41

And the congressional GOP is determined to slash public spending on programs that benefit ordinary Americans. This sets up confrontations through 2012 between congressional Republicans and President Obama, who must begin to sustain and raise revenues to reduce looming long-term deficits and support existing and newly promised benefits for the majority of Americans. At this point in U.S. history, any second New Deal involving redirection of federal interventions in an equality-enhancing direction is a much more fraught undertaking than an original New Deal—not least because there are no slack federal revenues available. Taxes and the budget will be at the center of domestic political conflicts for months and years to come.

HIDDEN POLICIES AND INVISIBLE REFORMS

Fighting for a second New Deal in the current U.S. policy and political landscape is also bound to be more confusing and opaque than the first New Deal because accretions of previous federal spending, regulations, and tax breaks crowd every major policy area—and large bureaucracies, multiple congressional committees, and hundreds of interest groups have a hand in ongoing policymaking in every realm. What is more, most recent policy changes have taken the form of hard-to-trace tax breaks and regulatory adjustments.

Back in the 1930s, American citizens could see that big, new things were being proposed and debated in Washington. Social Security at its inception was hard to miss: it enjoyed support from two-thirds or more beginning in the mid-1930s. As Social Security was implemented and expanded from the 1930s to the 1970s, its supporters could offer simple metaphors to try to make it popularly understandable. Direct benefit checks flowed to millions in due course, so Americans could understand where their payroll taxes had gone—to fund a program that makes a big difference for retirees and their children and grandchildren.

In contrast, today's U.S. public policies include many complex regulations and publicly invisible tax credits and tax breaks.[48] Political scientists Christopher Howard, Suzanne Mettler, and Jacob Hacker, among others, have chronicled the shift in recent decades toward the use of tax breaks and indirect "tax expenditures" for social policy purposes—and have shown how these mechanisms make the welfare state much less visible to ordinary citizens. Middle-class Americans enjoy much public support to buy houses, take out college loans, and obtain health care from employers that claim tax subsidies. But in all instances, they may not know that public policy matters a great deal to their personal and family fortunes. The "submerged state" is the term Mettler aptly uses to describe the network of regulations and subsidies that help so many without fostering commensurate citizen understanding.[49]

As exemplified by the Patient Protection and Affordable Care Act of 2010, major reforms nowadays impact already-mind-boggling complex sets of institutional arrangements—and necessarily turn into massive compilations of regulatory, tax, and spending provisions running to thousands of pages. Such complex measures are difficult for Congress-people to master, and virtually impossible to explain to citizens. People know that something big is being endlessly and bitterly argued about in Washington—but what is it? How can it be good, or workable? In the case of Affordable Care, citizens remain divided and puzzled long after the president signed the reform into law. Pollsters regularly tell us how many Americans "oppose" the health reform law, but they only occasionally mention that many of those opposed do not understand what the law includes, or does not include.

In short, already huge, pervasive, and complex government undertakings, many of them indirect benefits or barely visible tax breaks, are a challenge to rework—in highly partisan-polarized Washington. The complex policymaking involved makes it even more challenging for citizen majorities to appreciate what is going on than it would be if "all" that was happening was a tough battle like the one that occurred when Social Security was launched in the 1930s.

Given all of the difficulties the president and Democrats faced in 2009 and 2010, if we are just toting up legislative and regulatory accomplishments, the bills passed and decisions issued, Obama's ambitious agenda for policy change progressed quite remarkably—to institute comprehensive health reform, reform higher education loans, tighten regulation of financial institutions, and tweak many other realms of law and regulation. A new New Deal of sorts *was* successfully launched by President Obama and congressional Democrats in 2009 and 2010. But much of what happened was either invisible or ominously incomprehensible to the majority of American citizens. Big, worrisome, and easily caricatured—especially at a time of economic stress when people know one thing for sure: the national economy is not getting stronger fast enough to ensure that a rising tide lifts all boats. To advance major governmental reforms in such a context was an impressive accomplishment—but it was also a recipe for endless political controversy and electoral blowback.

The incomprehension and anxiety of everyday Americans have coexisted with acute awareness on the part of privileged strata and groups about even the smallest disadvantages imposed upon them by Obama's policy shifts. The slightest tweak in upper-end tax codes sets off a veritable explosion of political pushback. Business interests and many wealthy conservatives went all out to support GOP challengers to Democratic governors and congressional candidates in 2010—and are redoubling their efforts headed into November 2012. Ironically, the enemies of the cautious Obama New Deal knew what was up—even if they were more paranoid than actual policy changes justified. Established interests and conservatives understood that Obama and his Democratic allies were taking small steps that could have big social and political consequences over time, if they survived and were fully implemented. But the potential beneficiaries remained in the dark or were easily misled. Lower- and middle-income Americans could not see so clearly what was happening to federal policies they hardly understood; and of course they found it hard to imagine longer-term benefits from policy changes, like the Affordable Care Act, that will take many years to implement in full.

To put it mildly, this was not a winning political formula for the early Obama administration and its congressional Democratic allies, no matter how moderate or measured they endeavored to be in pursuing new legislation and regulations. Even a slight degree of redistribution toward the middle and lower strata seemed to be enough to generate determined opposition from the have-it-alls—who, of course, have ample resources of money and organizational clout to wage strong inside and outside political battles, including political advertising campaigns to turn wary voters against Democrats and their policy choices. Given the failure of the early economic recovery to gain sufficient steam to reemploy millions of out-of-work Americans, the Obama Democrats went into the November 2010 midterm election with discouraged supporters facing revved-up opponents. They faced Republican and conservative and business opponents determined to cut short and roll back early Obama reforms, while most Americans remained unsure that anything to their advantage had happened in Washington.

No wonder the Democrats lost in November 2010 even more resoundingly than routine U.S. political cycles suggested they might. The early Obama Democrats will go down in history as cautiously ambitious reformers who did just enough to provoke powerful enemies, while leaving their political friends, actual and potential, disappointed and mystified.

The Tea Party and the Radicalization of the GOP

So far, I have principally analyzed policy and politics during Obama's first years in the White House—because reformist presidents accomplish or launch much of what they will do at the start of their time in office. But perhaps the focus on President Obama and the Democrats of the 111th Congress is overblown. Years from now, in the cold light of retrospect, the main story of the critical juncture between 2008 and 2010, leading into the next round of U.S. electoral battles in 2012, may not be Barack Obama's hard-fought attempt at a second New Deal (even if key accomplishments like the Patient Protection and Affordable Care Act of 2010 survive in the long run). At least equally portentous, the remaking of the U.S. Republican Party, its extraordinary lunge toward antigovernment extremism, may turn out to be the headline. More than the usual cycles of U.S. politics have been at play in the GOP's repositioning at a juncture of dire national economic emergency. Even if the immediate propellants of the rightward lunge of the GOP under Obama wane, there are likely to be lasting reverberations from the turn of one of two major U.S. political parties toward outright obstruction of reforms and relentless bashing of government efforts to foster economic growth and social inclusion.

Much of the Republican Party's revival at the voting booth in 2010 was to be expected from the usual swings of U.S. elections exacerbated by a prolonged economic downturn. A Republican revival after 2008 was all the more in the cards given that pro-GOP constituencies were more likely to turn out in a midterm election. Nevertheless, if we do more than just register electoral margins, if we look at policy stances and national agendas of debate, it is clear that the 2010 Republican Party did not merely restore the pre-2008 status quo. The GOP circa 2011 is light years toward the right from the GOP circa 2000 or 2004. Partisan electoral swings in 2010 were both magnified and transformed by the eruption of the Tea Party. And the mobilization of grassroots activism and deployment of ultraconservative funding and ideological policy advocacy has remade the Republican Party, pledging its leaders to accelerate economic redistribution toward the very wealthy and reduce the role of the public sector in shaping economic growth and enhancing opportunity and security for middle- and lower-class Americans. If this remade GOP wins the presidency and both houses of Congress in 2012, the United States will experience radical policy shifts toward the right. Much of both the first New Deal and the Great Society will be dismantled, and the key Obama reforms of 2009 and 2010 will be repealed or gutted.

Tea Partyism in its various, loosely interlinked manifestations was able to rebrand and enormously energize hard-edged antigovernment conservatism, at once invigorating and repositioning the Republican Party heading into 2010.[50] Tea Party efforts promise to remain a force at least through the 2012 presidential contest. And in the meantime, Tea Party pressures will push GOPers in Washington and state capitals toward ever-more-obdurate refusal to compromise with President Obama and Democratic legislators. There may be cross-pressures from within and beyond the GOP, of course. But the Tea Party promises continued popular and elite momentum toward highly ideological hostility to the use of federal powers to promote economic growth and expand social opportunity. Tea Partiers are the anti–New Dealers of our time.

How did this happen? What exactly is the Tea Party, and why has it had such a big impact? What are likely to be the immediate and longer-term consequences of a radicalized, rightward-tugged GOP? These are the issues I tackle in this part of my analysis.

THE TEA PARTY ERUPTS AND GROWS

In late 2008 and early 2009, the tides of U.S. politics seemed to be running strongly against conservatives and the Republican Party. The November 2008 elections represented a triumph for an African American Democratic presidential candidate backed by strengthened congressional majorities and proposing ambitious and expensive federal initiatives for economic recovery and reform. Republicans were profoundly demoralized and fragmented, not only because of the election rout, but also because outgoing Republican president George W. Bush was so unpopular, the policies of his administration and party widely discredited.[51] Pundits declared the Republican Party in perhaps irreversible decline.[52] As of early 2009, the party seemed leaderless. The entourages of defeated GOP candidates John McCain and Sarah Palin were pointing recriminating fingers at one another, while Republican congressional leaders John Boehner and Mitch McConnell seemed to be grasping for tactical leverage.

Many American voters never liked Obama, of course. As he took office, conservatives in and around the Republican Party were angry and alarmed, strongly opposed to Obama and his policy initiatives. But how could a countermovement crystallize with the GOP in such disarray? In the first weeks of the new administration, opposition was scattered. Local protests opposed the American Recovery and Reinvestment Act (commonly called the Stimulus) and decried the bailouts of the banking sector and the Detroit auto companies. "Porkulus" was the favored term of derision, but it lacked punch as a rallying cry.

In mid-February of 2009, just weeks after Obama's inauguration, an inspiration presented itself. On February 19, CNBC financial commentator Rick Santelli, speaking from the floor of the Chicago Mercantile Exchange, launched a rant against nascent Obama administration policies to help underwater mortgage holders, many of them lower-income and minority Americans. By subsidizing "the losers' mortgages," Santelli proclaimed, the "government is rewarding bad behavior!" He invited America's "capitalists" to a "Chicago Tea Party" to protest this government intervention. His call invoked Revolutionary War symbolism and signified a revolt of authentic Americans against both overweening government and socially marginal freeloaders.

Across the country, web-savvy conservative activists recognized rhetorical gold when they saw it. Operating at first through the social-networking site Twitter, conservative bloggers and Republican campaign veterans took the opportunity offered by the Santelli rant to plan protests under the newly minted "Tea Party" name.[53] Instrumental to this early mobilization were loose networks organized around certain Twitter "hashtags"—the keywords Twitter users apply to tag the subject matter of their online comments—which allowed activists from a variety of different conservative networks to connect and combine forces. The video of the Santelli rant quickly scaled the media pyramid. It headlined the popular conservative website, *The Drudge Report;* was widely retelevised; and even provoked comment from the podium of White House press secretary Robert Gibbs. Indeed, Gibbs's heated comments directed specifically at Santelli gave the story additional media credibility and helped spread coverage of the Tea Party label.

On February 27, initial Tea Party protests drew small crowds in dozens of cities across the country. But the efforts persisted over the following weeks and months, with events featuring protesters with incendiary signs dressed up like Revolutionary-era patriots and waving tea bags to call to mind the original Boston Tea Party. Fox News amplified the public attention Tea Party groups were receiving, and connected their viewers with online tools to start or link up with their local Tea Party. Indeed, Vanessa Williamson's analysis of media coverage shows that, whereas other media outlets covered big, national Tea Party events when they happened, Fox News was out in front, offering steady "coverage" for weeks leading into each major event. And Fox acted as a kind of movement orchestrator, by offering models and contact information to local and regional viewers hoping to connect with one another to form ongoing networks. In these ways, Fox News actually served as a cheerleader for Tea Party events and helped otherwise scattered conservatives gain a sense of shared identity and pooled tactical knowledge.[54] After some months of growing Tea Party protests, mainstream media outlets became transfixed by the spectacle of older white protesters in colorful costumes engaged in outlandish attacks on Obama and federal policies. By 2010, the Tea Party was a featured story on all sorts of media platforms. Only a minority of Americans were involved or sympathetic, but the story line of older white protesters denouncing the nation's first black president was irresistible.

Quieter but crucial activities unfolded in many localities, where activists and concerned citizens went well beyond watching TV or traveling to the occasional big protest event. In communities scattered across every U.S. state, people started using MeetUp and other online tools to convene local meetings. During 2009 and 2010, more than 800 ongoing local Tea Party groups formed, meeting regularly in restaurants, churches, and other public venues. Local groups often sent carpools or busloads of "Patriots" to regional Tax Day protests, starting in mid-April 2009, as well as to national protests, such as the march on Washington on September 12, 2009, involving tens of thousands of Tea Party protesters. During 2010, self-declared Tea Party activists and supporters exercised significant clout in special elections and Republican primary contests. And once Tea Party forces started to matter in electoral contests, they became a permanent feature of national political coverage and commentary.

GRASSROOTS TEA PARTIERS

Who were the people inspired by the Tea Party label who threw themselves into protests and organizing? Observers debated this matter during 2009, and it took a while for a firm profile to emerge. In national polls, seemingly minor differences in question wording influenced early conclusions about the breadth of Tea Party affiliation, but in due course a depiction emerged from improved surveys and firsthand accounts of meetings and protests.[55] Older, white, and middle class is the typical profile of a Tea Party participant. Between 55 and 60 percent are men; 80 to 90 percent are white; and 70 to 75 percent are over 45 years old. Given the disproportionate number of older white males, it is little surprise that Tea Party people usually have somewhat higher incomes than typical Americans.

Demography alone is hardly decisive, though. Attitudes and political loyalties are much more important. The vast majority of Tea Party participants are conservative Republicans, many of whom have been politically active or very involved in community affairs in the past. A few polls have suggested that the Tea Party draws heavily from independent voters, but those studies neglected to add the standard follow-up question about whether respondents lean toward one party or another.[56] "Leaners" typically behave like party faithful, so polls omitting this question are likely overstating their respondents' party independence.[57] Self-styled Tea Party "independents," moreover, are often to the right of the GOP, more attracted to libertarian ideas and figures than to mainstream Republicanism. Polls conducted by Quinnipiac and Greenberg Quinlan Rosner, among a few others, include the relevant follow-up question, and find that three-quarters or more of Tea Party supporters are Republicans or lean Republican.[58] Tea Partiers do not see themselves as moderates. In June 2010, Gallup found that 62 percent of Tea Partiers deemed themselves to be conservative Republicans.[59]

Many Tea Partiers have been active in politics in the past, beyond the simple act of voting. The CBS News/*New York Times* survey found that 43 percent of Tea Party supporters nationwide claimed previously to have worked actively for a candidate or given money in a campaign. In the research my associates and I have done in Massachusetts, Virginia, and Arizona, we have talked with Tea Partiers previously active as GOP leaders, as advocates for religious conservative causes, as followers of Ron Paul, and, in one case, as a self-avowed "Bircher," a longtime adherent of the John Birch Society. While some Tea Partiers may be new to political activism, seasoned hands are by all indications more common in Tea Party ranks than in the U.S. citizenry as a whole.[60]

Tea Partiers have distinctive and shared media-consumption habits that allow them to be part of a community of meaning and emotion. Conservative media outlets have played a crucial role in forging the shared beliefs and the collective identity around which Tea Partiers have united. This community-building effort has been led by Fox News, with a strong assist from talk radio hosts and the conservative blogosphere. Fox is the primary source of political information for Tea Party activists. According to the CBS/*New York Times* national poll, 63 percent of Tea Party supporters watch Fox News, compared with 11 percent of all respondents. Only 11 percent of Tea Party supporters report getting their news from one of the Big Three networks, while among all U.S. respondents, more than a quarter reported watching network news.[61] Locally active Tea Partiers we have interviewed report the same kinds of media loyalties—above all to Fox News and conservative Internet sites. Local right-wing radio hosts, in turn, participate actively in many community Tea Party efforts.

What do Tea Partiers substantively believe and want? Hatred of "intrusions" by the federal government, fear of high and unsustainable levels of public spending, worries about tax hikes and a "disastrous" national deficit—all of these fiscal concerns are widely shared. Social issues also matter to many Tea Partiers, not just the long-standing Christian conservative concerns to combat abortion and block homosexual rights, but an almost obsessive level of worry about illegal immigration. We found that fear everywhere we looked in Tea Party circles, not just in Arizona, but also in New England. Another top Tea Party cause is blocking or dismantling regulations from federal bureaucracies such as the EPA or the FDA or the Education Department, and repealing "ObamaCare" (the 2010 health reform law).

Tea Partiers tend to be wary, even suspicious of elected politicians, but they reliably support Republicans against Democrats. The vast majority are not tempted to form or support a third party, for the purely pragmatic reason that such a move would advantage the Democratic Party—which Tea Partiers truly hate. They see Democrats as an unholy alliance of welfare recipients, unionized public employees, and politicians who are poised to grant citizenship to illegal immigrants in order to bolster their electoral prospects.

Pragmatically, Tea Partiers realize that they have to work to change the GOP and function through its candidates. Even so, they believe that all elected officials tend to lose sight of those who "sent them" to Washington or state capitals. Tea Party activists are not very amenable to the idea of delegated political authority, even when elected officeholders are at issue. They aim to keep a close eye on those they nominate or elect, to make sure they "follow the Constitution"—a document that grassroots Tea Partiers tend to believe is self-evident to all in its meanings. Tea Party people repeatedly say they will work against GOP officials in the next election, if those officials do not heed the "will of the people." They do not mean they will vote for Democrats; they mean they will mount challenges in GOP primaries.

My research partners and I have used personal interviews to probe the nuances of Tea Party views about the core functions of government. Commentators seem to take it for granted that Tea Party people are consistently opposed to all kinds of federal government spending and taxation, and assume that Tea Partiers are just pushing for less government overall. All-out opposition to government spending seems evident from Tea Party signs in public rallies, and in findings from national polls that pose very broad, zero-sum alternatives. Simple antigovernment priorities also seem evident in the declarations of leading Republican politicians or national advocacy groups that claim to speak for "the Tea Party." But our research team was skeptical from the start because, after all, the U.S. federal spending is overwhelmingly channeled to national defense, military veterans' benefits, Medicare, and Social Security. How plausible is it that older, white Americans are unequivocally opposed to a national government that primarily does these things?

GOOD AND BAD GOVERNMENT SPENDING

To get beyond public slogans and general polling, my research collaborators and I have conducted in-depth interviews with grassroots Tea Party participants in eastern Massachusetts, in two places around Phoenix, Arizona, and in southeastern and central Virginia. State activists vary to some degree: Arizonans emphasize state autonomy and gun rights; Virginians meld Christian conservative rhetoric and practices with Tea Party libertarianism; and Tea Partiers in Massachusetts tend to be secular in orientation. Yet everywhere we went to meet grassroots Tea Partiers, we found older whites with similar very conservative views—probably because they all share media-viewing habits and are part of a national political community. What is more, all the Tea Partiers we engaged offered much more nuanced views about government programs and public spending than might seem apparent from public stereotypes.[62]

In discussions with regular Tea Party participants, we have learned that many are glad to acknowledge receipt of Medicare, Social Security, or veterans' benefits. They know they are getting publicly funded benefits, and feel perfectly entitled to them. One Tea Party woman we spoke to declared that she would not take Social Security and Medicare when she retires, in order to be consistent about fighting the deficit and slashing federal spending. But that is unusual. Most grassroots Tea Party people want these programs to be available for others in the future, as well as for themselves. In Tea Party eyes, there clearly are important things the federal government does—including care for veterans along with the dispensation of Medicare and Social Security. Many are ready to support taxation for such worthwhile programs.

A recent poll, for example, explicitly asked a national sample of Americans whether they would support lifting the cap on wages subject to the Social Security payroll tax in order to preserve benefits in the future. Seventy-seven percent of all Americans said yes, compared to 10 percent who wanted to hold the line on the tax and cut benefits. Within this overall picture of very strong support for Social Security, Americans who say they support the Tea Party were only slightly different from the norms for all others across age categories, income levels, and partisan lines. Sixty-seven percent of Tea Partiers supported raising the payroll tax to sustain Social Security, compared to only 20 percent who preferred benefit reductions. This national poll result makes sense given what we heard in personal conversations. To Tea Party men and women who collect benefits for military veterans or are enrolled in Medicare and Social Security, involvement with governmentally managed social provision does not seem illegitimate.

How can this be? It is easily explained when we grasp how Tea Partiers, like many other Americans, understand legitimate social spending. Tea Party beneficiaries feel they have "paid for" the federal benefits they receive—and they do not just mean "paid" in monetary terms. In heartfelt responses, they stress their lifetimes of work and paying taxes. Such contributions, they say, set them and other true Americans apart from "freeloaders" whose claim to public benefits the Tea Partiers consider they have not "paid for." Again, more than finances are involved because "freeloaders," in the Tea Party view, are people who collect benefits they have not paid for, ripping off regular American taxpayers. Who are these "freeloaders"? Certain categories of people came up again and again in the examples and stories people recounted. Racial minorities, immigrants, and younger people are the types of people who appear again and again.

Immigrants, including illegals, are seen not so much as a threat to U.S. jobs as a threat to the public fisc. Immigrants are fingered by Tea Partiers as likely to make claims on welfare and public services that will have to be funded by longtime hard-working Americans like themselves. (The fact that youthful immigrants, legal and illegal, actually strengthen Social Security for today's older citizens by contributing payroll taxes, often without building legal entitlement to benefits, is lost on Tea Party people.) In addition, many Tea Partiers mentioned irresponsible younger people as folks likely to "freeload," including students who use Pell grants or collect Food Stamps while they study. So deep do intergenerational worries run, in fact, that our informants sometimes gave us examples of younger people in their own families who do not hold down regular jobs and feel entitled to collect "something for nothing" from public programs.

Tea Partiers, in short, fear *new kinds* of federal government spending, and expansions of government welfare or social services, that might go to less worthy categories of people, including low-income persons, immigrants, and irresponsible young folks. People of color are often referenced implicitly, but the tension about immigrants seems even greater than resentment of African Americans. In any event, in Tea Party eyes, public spending for freeloading people seems morally illegitimate because they have not "earned their way" through hard work. Increases in such spending—including the sorts of increases that have happened relatively automatically to help those thrown out of employment in the Great Recession—also seem threatening to Tea Partiers because they worry that worthy Americans like themselves will have to pay higher taxes to fund illegitimate entitlements and save profligate governments from bankruptcy.

In their way of thinking, therefore, Tea Partiers are not being illogical in supporting and accepting Medicare and

Social Security at the same time they hate the Affordable Care Act of 2010. In point of fact, Affordable Care promises to tax the wealthy and trim the most luxurious Medicare plans to pay for Medicaid expansions for lower-income people and fund federal subsidies to make private health insurance affordable for lower-and middle-income Americans.[63] Tea Partiers see Obama's health reform as a form of welfare, as one more example of a "Democrat" program to tax real Americans to help the less worthy. "Redistribute my work ethic!" declared a telltale sign at a Boston Tea Party rally. Or, as a typical Tea Party bumper sticker puts it: "Keep Working. Millions on Welfare are Counting on You." Tea Partiers are the self-styled "real Americans" whose work, present or past (after all, many are retirees), earned them their public benefits. Social Security, Medicare, and veterans' benefits are essential and legitimate in their eyes—so they are hardly opposed to vast chunks of what the federal government spends now, or will spend in the future. But Tea Partiers do not want their work or wealth tapped to pay for benefits for other Americans (or illegal immigrants) whom they see as unworthy and undeserving. They have no sympathy for people they think are "not paying their own way."

These sentiments—setting legitimate recipients of public benefits against undeserving "freeloaders"—are long-standing staples of populist conservatism in the United States. Tea Party resentments are just the latest versions of opposition to (real or perceived) *redistribution* through federal expenditures and taxation. Right now, moreover, it is not surprising that there is a generational as well as ethnic and racial edge to long-standing kinds of conservative resentment. After all, the Great Recession was a financially fueled downturn that abruptly undercut pensions and home values, the embodiments of lifetimes of effort and modest wealth accumulation for many older Americans. Meanwhile, younger people are having an even harder time than in recent decades getting into the labor market, forming families, buying homes. Tea Partiers feel economically stressed, and they look out to see youngsters behaving in ways they find puzzling or offensive. Structural changes in the U.S. economy exacerbate the usual ways in which the young seem irresponsible to the old.

In addition, immigrant flows since 1965 have brought many more people of color into U.S. society. And both native-born and immigrant black and brown people make up a higher share of younger U.S. cohorts. Add all of the foregoing up, and it is easy to see why older white people, including the Tea Partiers in their ranks, are witnessing societal changes that may seem threatening. America is changing in ways they do not recognize, in ways they do not want government to support or facilitate. "I want my country back" is the oft-repeated refrain of Tea Partiers for good reason. At the grass-roots, Tea Partyism is a restorationist movement.

Against the backdrop of their views and perspectives on society, it is easy to understand why President Obama is universally hated by Tea Partiers. "Hatred" is a word they often use, or its equivalents, so I am not unfairly attributing the sentiment. And of course, the Tea Party erupted at the grass roots only after the new Democratic president took office. Tea Party people we have talked with explain that Obama's ascension to office was the straw that broke the camel's back, the blow that spurred them to reactive counter-organization. Commentators trying to be purely logical often point out that the federal government ran up large deficits and increased spending well before 2008—and our Tea Party informants always note this, too. So why didn't the Tea Party happen while Republicans were in D.C.? In a way, knowing that Tea Partiers are overwhelmingly conservative Republicans, or people to the right of the GOP, answers this question. Future Tea Partiers resented many policy moves taken in the Bush era, but held their anger in check—and certainly did not want to support Democrats. However, there is more going on since 2008. Obama's arrival in the White House was symbolically explosive.

Given what people have said to us, here is what makes sense. For older white Tea Partiers, it was shocking to see someone named "Barack Hussein Obama" in office, and the man himself readily embodies all the societal changes that make them anxious. As one Boston participant told us, "I just can't relate to him." Obama is a relatively young Democratic president—and, to boot, a black man fathered by a foreigner. Obama's "fired up and ready to go" base of support in 2008 included millions of enthusiastic younger voters, as well as black and brown Americans in high proportions. Given the coincidence of Obama's reform promises with the economic shock of the Great Recession, this president launched aggressive federal measures that can seem very threatening to people who are experiencing losses in wealth and who worry that federal benefits to which they are already entitled may be crowded out or undercut by expensive new federal undertakings.

Obama the man, Obama the electoral phenomenon, and Obama the policymaker together add up to the "perfect storm" of threat from the perspective of older, white, conservative Republicans. No wonder many of them erupted in 2009—and clearly their protests are not about "federal spending" or "deficits" in general. Their anger reacts to the possibility that federal spending and taxes could shift in favor of younger Americans, including many black and brown people. Any such development would have been worrisome to the kinds of people who participate in the Tea Party no matter what the economy was like in 2009 and 2010. But the threat heightened when we add in the Great Recession's impact on pensions and home values, the possibility of taxes on folks like them or cuts in their benefits being used for redistributive programs like Affordable Care, and the threat the growing federal deficit could pose to elderly entitlements. No wonder early 2009 turned out to be the moment for the Tea Party to erupt among otherwise discouraged conservative Republicans. Obama and his administration were just too much—and the new president and his Democratic allies were perfect targets for political wrath and mobilization.

ORGANIZED FROM THE BOTTOM UP— AND THE TOP DOWN

Debates about the Tea Party focus not only on who participants are demographically and attitudinally but also on the organization of the phenomenon. Although made up of conservative Republicans, the Tea Party as such has not been directly formed or operated through established GOP organs— not through the Republican National Committee or through state GOP organizations. Nor are official GOP party leaders or elected officials in any simple sense "in control" of Tea Party activities or goals. The Tea Party consists of Republican voters and, often, experienced GOP activists. And it aims to influence and use the Republican Party. But it was not created by the GOP, and it is not directly controlled by establishment Republicans.

Debates among observers have focused on whether the Tea Party is a top-down or bottom-up undertaking. Many on the left argue that the Tea Party is an "AstroTurf" phenomenon incited and puffed up by big money operators and Fox News—essentially seeing it as a relabeled coterie of the usual suspects in the right-wing big-money firmament. Conservative observers, meanwhile, romanticize the Tea Party as a purely grassroots social movement, which is said to have drawn new, previously apolitical people into politics, with all of the energy and effort coming from below.

My collaborators and I find this either/or debate to be misguided. According to our research and analysis, what makes the Tea Party so effective and dynamic is a mutually reinforcing combination of bottom-up and top-down undertakings. The Tea Party itself is not one organization, not even a single unified network. It is rather a loosely interconnected field of networks and organizations, only occasionally crystallized into more coordinated undertakings. A tripartite mix of local grassroots networks, resource-deploying national organizations, and conservative media outlets constitute the Tea Party overall. The dynamic interplay of grassroots activists, national advocates, and media impresarios has given the Tea Party its oomph, allowing it to fuel and move the Republican Party, as well as national political debates, well toward the right.

From the bottom up, Tea Parties are small, loosely interrelated networks, assembled at the initiative of local and regional organizers, who often use online organizing tools. The website MeetUp, which helps people with given interests identify one another and arrange face-to-face meetings, has been very widely used by Tea Partiers and can give us some sense of the phenomenon's breadth and depth. As of July 2010, sixteen Tea Party groups listed on MeetUp had more than 500 members; seven of these groups were in Florida and four were in Texas. About 250 other Tea Party MeetUp groups had more than 100 members, and there were several hundred other, smaller Tea Party groups. On a typical day, MeetUp listed about twenty Tea Party events nationwide—including rallies, seminars, candidate fundraisers, and casual events such as barbeques or book club meetings. These results from MeetUp are in keeping with an October 2010 *Washington Post* investigation, which found a total of about 650 Tea Parties, many of which were not very active.[64] By the late spring of 2011, our research team used websites to document more than 800 active Tea Parties spread across all fifty states.[65] The groups claiming the largest online lists of members—people who keep in touch, even if they only occasionally attend monthly meetings—were to be found in state capitals and in the southern states where Republicans are especially strong.

Local groups of Tea Partiers do quite a lot, engaging in various related efforts at multiple levels of politics.[66] Like a local group of Patriots we observed in Virginia, many local groups meet regularly to hear lectures, engage in training to do electoral politics, and discuss issues. Participants may end up socializing with one another outside of the meetings as such. Some of them mobilize to take over local GOP committees. And Tea Partiers may carpool or ride buses to participate in regional, state, or national protests or—increasingly, as time goes by—to lobby their elected officials on behalf of Tea Party priorities or to express anger and fear about "Obama-Care" or other federal policies.

In the state of Virginia, Tea Party organization has reached a new height because there is a state-level federation that held a major convention in Richmond in the fall of 2010.[67] The Virginia Tea Party Federation has elected leaders and organizes "lobby days" at the legislature; it also convenes the leaders of several dozen local Tea Party groups for weekly conference calls to keep in touch and coordinate activities. Although a few other states, most notably Michigan, show signs of significant state-level organization, Virginia seems to be on the high end of autonomous organizational elaboration, in which local and state activities are linked. Virginia is a swing state, with Tea Party–friendly officials in state office, and parts of the state are close enough to Washington to allow activists to take "day trips" to meet with Congresswoman Michele Bachmann or Senator Jim DeMint, organizers of Tea Party caucuses in the U.S. House and Senate, respectively. Virginia Tea Partiers, in short, face a welcoming political opportunity structure, and one that encourages coordination across national, state, and local levels of action. Even if it is unusually well-developed, the Virginia Tea Party Federation shows what might be possible—although, in our observation, local Tea Partiers are anxious to preserve their autonomy and will not easily join higher-level federated arrangements.

Given the findings of our research and the 2010 *Washington Post* survey looking for clearly active local groups, the extent and size of grassroots Tea Party undertakings seem both substantial and somewhat smaller than the constant drumbeat of national media attention might lead one to believe. To understand how loosely interconnected small groups have made such a large impact on the political scene, we must also look upward, and understand the network of well-funded national advocacy organizations promoting the Tea Party brand.

At the national level there is no unified, official Tea Party organization, but many would-be leaders and organizations have tried to stoke and capitalize on grassroots fervor. National orchestrators draw their resources from a small number of very conservative business elites, whose long-standing policy concerns primarily involve reducing government oversight and regulation and shrinking or radically restructuring broad social entitlements in the United States.[68] Again, Obama's election with Democratic majorities in Congress did not create these forces or change their goals. But, certainly, antigovernment conservative funders and national advocacy groups were galvanized to push back hard at the threat of a possible second New Deal that Obama posed, in their eyes, should his policies prove successful, popular, and sustainable.

Two advocacy organizations have become most closely associated with the Tea Party name: the Tea Party Express (TPE) and Tea Party Patriots (TPP).[69] The TPE is a project of the Republican-run political action committee (PAC) Our Country Deserves Better, which has provided hundreds of thousands of dollars in support to conservative candidates like Senator Scott Brown in Massachusetts and Sharron Angle in Nevada. The TPE also channeled big money into Republican primaries.[70] Beyond these electoral activities, the TPE has sponsored bus tours that travel the country and coincide with other Tea Party events. Tea Party Patriots, whose website was up and running within days of the original Santelli rant, has been more closely associated with grassroots activism than TPE. Many Tea Party groups have registered on the TPP website, and, according to TPP national coordinator Jenny Beth Martin, the organization employs nine national coordinators to help guide and coordinate these local groups' actions.[71] The weekly phone conferences and state websites that help local groups engage in federated cooperation have been encouraged by TPP and may have been funded from its coffers.

TPP rhetoric and the group's homespun website give the impression of an entirely grassroots, volunteer-run organization. Jenny Beth Martin derides the TPE as "five people on a bus," and her TPP dubs itself the "official grassroots American movement." As of October 2010, the TPP website offered the visitor no information regarding their national leadership and no listing of the board of directors or staff. Nonetheless, TPP is very closely intertwined with Freedom-Works, a multimillion-dollar conservative nonprofit led by former House majority leader Dick Armey (R-TX). TPP operates under the motto "Fiscal Responsibility, Limited Government, Free Market," similar to the FreedomWorks slogan of "Lower Taxes, Less Government, More Freedom." As Jenny Beth Martin acknowledges, FreedomWorks was crucial to the group's original launch and was a primary funder for its national rallies. Martin also reports that operational funding for TPP was scant well into 2010, limiting the capacity of the group to take independent action.[72] Leaked emails have suggested that, at least in early months, FreedomWorks retained control over significant aspects of TPP messaging.[73]

TPE, TPP, and FreedomWorks are not the only Tea Party–linked national conservative organizations. Other prominent right-wing advocacy organizations fishing in these waters include Americans for Prosperity, an advocacy group that, like FreedomWorks, is a spin-off of the 1980s free-market, industry-funded think tank Citizens for a Sound Economy; Newt Gingrich's American Solutions for Winning the Future; and the American Liberty Alliance, an organization run by the conservative campaign veteran Eric Odom. Several of these organizations, along with right-wing think tanks like the Heritage Foundation and the Cato Institute, have been bankrolled by a small number of far-right businessmen, most notably the libertarian Koch brothers, sons of Fred Koch, a founding member of the John Birch Society.[74] Thus the national organizations promoting the Tea Party are most closely tied to ultra-free-market, pro-business conservatism, rather than church-linked social conservatism.

It is not clear how much many grassroots Tea Partiers know about the national advocacy and funding organizations promoting and trying to capitalize on their efforts. Many activists my associates and I have interviewed know little or nothing about FreedomWorks or the other national free-market organizations promoting the Tea Party brand. Other local people, especially organizers who set up Tea Party websites or arrange for outside speakers to come to monthly meetings, are more familiar with national and state-level advocacy groups that may provide help and resources. The relationship between local Tea Parties and national advocacy organizations and PACs is not one of simple "control" from either top or bottom. Mutual leverage is a better way to understand what is going on. Grassroots groups get occasional encouragement and infusions of resources from national organizations—free visiting speakers, a bus to take people to rallies, links on local websites to national ideological organizations, grants to help set up a website, and so forth. At the same time, national, professionally run right-wing organizations use local activism as a colorful backdrop, and milk contacts with local activists to build their email lists and enhance the legitimacy of the policy proposals they push on Republican officeholders and candidates. National funders who have linked their fortunes to the "Tea Party" also use the movement to raise funds and channel contributions into election campaigns, to influence both Republican primaries and general contests. Finally, the third big force in the Tea Party firmament, the conservative media complex centered on Fox News, also benefits from grassroots and elite Tea Party efforts, and furthers them by providing sustained favorable coverage.

Overall, links among the Tea Party forces—elite organizations, media, and grassroots groups—are loose and mutually back scratching, not hierarchical or controlling. Yet the Tea Party phenomenon as a whole has benefited strategically from the looseness of these ties. The Tea Party is all about boosting the GOP and pushing it rightward. Elites, grassroots, and conservative media leaders are all trying to do that. Because there is no one center or obvious source of authority and resources, the fate of Tea Party enthusiasm, or even the fate of Tea Party funding efforts, is not inextricably linked to the political fortunes of any one candidate or entity. Grassroots engagement is not undercut when particular candidates are defeated or particular organizations are discredited.

Similarly, national actors such as FreedomWorks or Fox News do not have to be accountable to actual participants. Elites who want to leverage grassroots mobilizations—for example, to influence a GOP primary election contest—are free to inject millions of dollars into advertising or voter contact efforts, without having to go through any cumbersome process of hearing popular views or dealing directly with local network leaders. Advocacy groups that want to destroy Social Security can speak in the name of local activists who, mostly, support Social Security! And it also works organizationally. Grassroots Tea Partiers are not likely to say "no" if they get resources for buses to demonstrations or to set up a website, so the outside funders do not usually alienate them. Yet the outside funders can pick and choose where they deploy major resources, and they can hog the media spotlight when reporters want colorful stories or need someone to speak for "the Tea Party." This gives the top-down impresarios in the Tea Party universe considerable leverage, without the bother of democratic accountability.

PUSHING THE GOP TOWARD THE ANTIGOVERNMENT RIGHT

Although the Tea Party is not tightly coordinated or centrally directed, it does pay high dividends to wealthy right-wing elites who have, for some time, worked to push the GOP toward the right, especially on issues involving taxes or business regulation. The Club for Growth, for example, has been active for years, channeling money to conservative primary challengers whenever necessary to prevent Republicans from agreeing to tax increases or engaging in compromise with Democrats on fiscal or regulatory matters. But until the Tea Party, right-wing pro-business, antigovernment elites relied on funneling money for elections and media campaigns. They did not have organized grassroots activists. The conservative grass roots were, on the whole, organized by Christian right leaders with their own autonomous networks and goals and values somewhat tangential to the ultra-free-market elites.

Now the free-marketers have direct reach into localities and regions. With the assistance of the conservative media's inspiration of willing local activists and participants, the antiregulation big-business lobby can harness new grassroots networks to accompany their already-powerful D.C. presence. By mid-2010, the Tea Party—though never involving more than a minority of all Americans—could mount spectacular regional and national protests and attract the attention of mainstream media and the political class in Washington. It also intervened dramatically in many GOP primaries.

Throughout the primary season leading into the November 2010 elections, Tea Party money people and grassroots activists coordinated to deliver one-two punches against Republican contenders, including longtime D.C. incumbents, who were deemed too moderate, too willing to compromise with the Obama administration or Democrats in Congress. Utah's Republican senator Bob Bennett was defeated in a caucus-based primary by Mike Lee, an ultraconservative, Tea Party candidate. Bennett's sin? He had cosponsored some legislation with Senate Democrats. Tea Party activists and funders also combined to fuel Rand Paul in Kentucky, who won the right to contest the general election by defeating the handpicked establishment Republican favored by GOP minority leader Senator Mitch McConnell. Alaska's GOP incumbent Lisa Murkowski was challenged by an extreme right-wing Tea Party candidate, Joe Miller, who received huge infusions of cash from the California-based TPE. Express billionaires also sent money into the GOP Delaware primary to help Christine O'Donnell mobilize her southern Delaware grassroots base to defeat moderate Republican Mike Castle.

Mention of these instances tells us that Tea Party efforts—by which we mean the loose intercalation of local grassroots activism and infusions of millions of dollars of funding across state lines into selected contexts—did not always produce general election victories in 2010, not even in a midterm election where older, richer, white voters were a disproportionate presence. In states that were safe for the GOP, a Tea Party challenger could displace a mainstream conservative Republican without risking loss in November 2010. But in Delaware, Colorado, Alaska, and Nevada, the intra-GOP Tea Party victory turned to dross when Democrats won enough middle-of-the-road voters to win in November.[75]

However, the impact of the Tea Party on GOP dynamics and the party's policy agenda remains strong, even though some seats that might have been added to GOP Senate ranks were lost in 2010. Successful primary challenges from the right send powerful messages to GOP officeholders and would-be candidates, causing them to guard their flank by trying to toe the line on issues the activists are highlighting. Who imagines that Indiana's Dick Lugar, up for reelection in 2012, will make any moves to cooperate with Democrats on fiscal or business issues in the 112th Congress? He won't, because his state has fired-up Tea Party activists, a minority of a minority party, to be sure, but active and attentive all the same; and Lugar also knows that billionaire Tea Party funders are intervening in his state's media markets with negative ads. Similar dynamics are at work for Senator Orrin Hatch of Utah. In total, the 112th Congress has moved sharply to the right because of popular and elite Tea Party efforts. Republican leaders are determined to keep confronting and obstructing President Obama and the Democrats all the way through 2012, and they can easily use Tea Party threats to help keep any would-be GOP moderates or compromises under control.

We have seen how anger among increasingly well-organized grassroots Tea Partiers, plus the determination of Tea Party funders to shift the D.C. status quo, came together to help magnify the anti-Democratic tides in the 2010 election contests. Intensity of efforts increased among the very groups of voters more likely to turn out in opposition to the Democrats in the midterm election. And in the wake of the Tea Party upsurge and the *Citizens United* decision removing controls on fundraising, the 2010 contests were also inviting for elites looking not just to unseat Democrats but also to tug Republicans toward free-market, low-tax policies. So the Tea Party helps us understand the blowbacks against what was otherwise a moderate Obama reform agenda during 2009 and 2010.

Since January 2011, Tea Party caucuses in Congress, along with ever-more-ramified and better-organized Tea Party activism in many key states, have pushed GOP officials in Washington and the states toward extraordinary efforts to slash public workforces and cut public spending, while at the same time pressing steadily for further deregulation of business and generous tax breaks for the well-to-do. The Republican Party is now positioned well to the right of the Republican Party of the early 2000s under President George W. Bush. In essence, today's GOP is doubling down on policies that many observers of all stripes believe helped to cause the economic meltdown of 2008 and balloon the federal deficits in recent years. This is a truly remarkable state of affairs for one of America's two erstwhile mainstream political parties.

Much of the remarkable GOP rightward shift is attributable to the direct and indirect effects of Tea Party activists and funders—to the leverage their interrelated efforts have created around the rightward edges of the Republican Party in the age of Obama. Conservatives used the Tea Party inspiration to marshal their forces against Obama's New Deal starting early in 2009, not just to oppose Democrats but also to pressure Republicans never to compromise with Democratic preferences. Tea Partiers may be less prominent in the media as the Republican Party nominates a presidential candidate and seeks to appear more centrist heading into November 2012. But grassroots and elite Tea Party activists are still hard at work. They will turn out and give money with enthusiasm to fight Obama's reelection, and they will not stop harrying and obstructing the president until November 2012, when they hope to dump him into the dust bin of history.

A Contentious Future for American Politics

The first part of my analysis probed the accomplishments, shortfalls, and unintended political effects of President Obama's effort to fashion a second New Deal, to revise U.S. taxes and social programs to redress inequalities and expand social opportunity and security. The second part traced the origins, characteristics, and impact of the Tea Party—which has reacted against Obama's initiatives with a ferocity rarely seen in recent U.S. politics. Now let me conclude by speculating on the near-term and longer-term impacts of the dizzying turnarounds we have seen in U.S. politics over the past several years.

In late 2010, the rancor of the November election season receded for a time, as President Obama and the lame duck 112th Congress managed to enact a few final pieces of legislation. With enhanced Republican ranks looming, lame-duck congressional Democrats compromised about taxes on GOP terms—all the Bush-era cuts, including those for the very rich that Obama had promised to end, were continued through 2012. The waning 111th Congress managed to attract enough Republican votes in the Senate to approve two Obama priorities: an arms treaty with Russia; and ending "Don't ask, don't tell" barring openly gay people from military service. But along with the settlement of taxes on basically Republican terms, Obama had to accept defeat on the federal budget.

An intricately compromised budget for the next cycle was scrapped after Tea Party protests induced Republicans to back out of agreements and block a vote in the Senate. The government was kept going through a temporary fix, and new battles over the budget loomed for 2011—battles about yearly federal budgets and, most explosive of all, battles over what used to be routine legislation to raise the federal debt limit, that is, to allow the federal government to borrow to meet obligations Congress has already enacted. Month after month, culminating in a major crisis during the summer of 2011, radicalized Republicans threatened to stop allowing the United States to meet its obligations—a threat that, if carried through, would spur a worldwide financial crisis and actually increase the future indebtedness of the United States. No matter; Tea Party–oriented Republicans hoped to use this threat to force huge, immediate reductions in federal spending, especially on social programs for the American majority.

REPUBLICAN POLITICAL THEATER

As this overview of ongoing budget clashes underlines, the near-term consequences of the major shifts toward a rightward-leaning GOP became instantly obvious with the arrival of the 112th Congress in January 2011. GOPer John

Boehner took over as Speaker of the House, with a Republican contingent that was both very large and ideologically positioned further to the right than any previous House since political scientists started measuring such things many decades ago.[76] Whatever compromises happened and will happen along the way between President Obama and congressional Republicans in 2011 and 2012—and both sides will occasionally need to compromise to get unavoidable matters settled—the country is in for D.C. political fireworks, more heat than light, more talk than action, at least through the 2012 election and probably long after. The stakes are high, but will not be immediately settled. The turnarounds of the 2008 and 2010 elections have mobilized partisans on both sides, especially at the rightward edge of the GOP. Divided government and compromises will not satisfy Tea Partiers or right-wing billionaires. They want it all—the full repeal of health care reform and financial regulations accomplished during Obama's first two years; the full dismantling of regulations touching industries involved in health care, energy production, and financial services; the defunding and privatization of social entitlements for the poor and the vast American middle class; and, above all, huge cuts in the already modest taxes paid by billionaires, millionaires, and corporations. The GOP budget issued in April 2011 by Congressman Paul Ryan, chair of the Budget Committee, outlined just such a radical right-wing wish list.[77] Heading into November 2012, the Republican Party will press this agenda—especially the parts featuring tax cuts for businesses and the wealthy. Republicans are trying to position themselves for a total conservative triumph in 2013 and beyond.

It is not just me saying this. Republican Party leaders inside and outside government make little secret of their primary goal: defeat Obama in 2012 and install a GOP president and Congress to push through radical policy redirections. Earlier, I argued that GOP strategies after 2008 looked toward the next election, that decisions about what to accept or obstruct in Congress were taken with an eye to setting up contrasts, mobilizing supporters, and winning big in November 2010. Tea Party actions were also, in key respects, meant to discipline GOPers in office and keep them from reaching across the aisle. GOP and Tea Party tactics worked going into 2010, and the earlier victories tempt conservative leaders to try another round of the same tactics for 2012 (even though the electorate will be larger and more diverse in a presidential election year than it was in 2010). Because twenty-three Democratic Senate seats are at stake in 2012, with only ten GOP seats on the line, the Republicans know they may claim a small Senate majority in the 113th Congress, which will convene in January 2013. Republicans currently in the Senate will be emboldened to set up issues for resolution after that shift occurs; and Republicans planning to run for Senate seats also have a stake in mobilizing partisans for 2012. In the House of Representatives, even if substantial bounce back toward Democrats occurs in 2012, House Republicans are likely to maintain control, if only because redistricting after the 2010 census may make it easier for them to consolidate seats they took in 2010. The 2012 presidential contest and political battles leading into it thus become unusually consequential for a Republican Party—and for free-market advocates who hope not just to shift policy directions on the margins, but to roll back U.S. social programs and establish a long-term regime of low taxes and minimum government regulation of the economy.

The first major initiative of the Republican-controlled House in 2011 was a vote for lock-stock-and-barrel repeal of Obama's key New Deal–type accomplishment, the Affordable Care Act of 2010. This GOP repeal vote was not a governing step—after all, the legislation goes nowhere in the current Senate and President Obama has veto power. Nevertheless, John Boehner's House took this aggressive step quickly because "political theater," as commentators derisively labeled the effort, is the whole point. Tea Partiers are determined to get rid of "ObamaCare" and substantial majorities of Republican voters want repeal. The House GOP was fulfilling a promise made during the 2010 election to its base. But that was not all. The intention was to signal ongoing guerrilla warfare, to set up an unending series of dramatizations of GOP opposition to Affordable Care right up to the 2012 elections. Arguably, the repeal vote was a clear statement that the GOP no longer believes that the United States should do anything to extend health coverage to up to fifty million uninsured people, or anything at the national level to control rising health costs. The policy goal, to the degree there is one, is to go back to the pre-Obama status quo, and loosen existing state regulations of private insurers. But policymaking, or even unmaking, is not really the point. Stoking partisan anger and public doubts about Affordable Care is the plan, in order to set up issues for 2012. Obstruct implementation in the meantime, if possible. The argument to funders and voters is: Elect a Republican Senate and president to join with the Republican House in actually repealing "ObamaCare."

The same kind of strategy, featuring guerrilla warfare and political theater, is being pursued by the House GOP majority and the Senate GOP minority on budgetary and tax matters, indeed on any matter that can be portrayed as "big government" regulation of business. Why not continue a strategy that worked for Republicans between 2008 and 2010? That surely is what GOP congressional leaders think. Many Republican presidential candidates will likewise draw maximum contrasts with Obama and the Democrats—although some of them, like Mitt Romney, may simply hammer Obama on slow economic growth, hoping to set up a 2012 general election contest in which Republicans and Independents jointly vote to deny a second term to Obama, rather than looking too closely at what Republicans have done, or would do, on major policies. Congressional Republicans, in short, will keep the hard-core conservative base engaged, while the GOP presidential candidate fudges policy stands enough to appeal to middle-of-the-road voters who disapprove of Obama's handling of the national economy but do not buy what radicalized Republicans are offering in key states or at the national level. Whether this two-track Republican approach works depends on the course of economic growth and job creation through October.

A PRESIDENT WHO MUST SCORE ON DEFENSE

While GOPers chip away at previous policy accomplishments and try to set up bolder rollbacks after 2012, President Obama will not be able to pursue more of his original agenda for a second New Deal. Democrats will continue to talk about immigration reform, but there will not be action as long as Republicans control the House by a wide margin. Legislation on energy and the environment cannot pass, so Obama's White House will not push for it. The time for major legislative breakthroughs has come and gone—at least until after a possible Obama reelection in 2012. If Obama is reelected, bipartisan compromises on major legislation might become possible, assuming that Republicans hold the House and Senate by narrow margins. Under that scenario, incentives could shift slightly—for example, allowing elements of both parties to broker tradeoffs on immigration issues as well as on taxes and spending.

Whatever happens afterward, Obama must defend his landmark legislative accomplishments, trying to preserve his halfway New Deal, while tending to administrative implementation in a highly contentious environment. Republican congressional committees will keep harassing his executive appointees and lugging them into hearing after hearing, looking for scandals and hot-button issues to dramatize. Republican budget-makers will again and again seek to de-fund administrative agencies involved in implementing health, education, and financial reforms. Budget showdowns will continue to happen.

The president is far from powerless, though. Freed from the need to work out legislative bargains with congressional chambers both held by his own party, Obama can use the bully pulpit of the presidency to frame issues and influence public perceptions of what is going on, or not, in Washington. He used the bully pulpit repeatedly in 2011—to memorialize the dead and wounded in the attacks on Congresswoman Gabrielle Giffords's "Congress on Your Corner" event in Tucson, Arizona; to articulate the economic theme of "winning the future" in the 2011 State of the Union address; to criticize the Ryan GOP budget and lay out his own approach to addressing the federal deficit with a mix of taxes and spending cuts; to announce the killing of Osama bin Laden and a plan for troop withdrawals from Afghanistan. Starting in the late summer of 2011, after high-stakes negotiations led to the lifting of the debt ceiling by Congress, President Obama turned to public advocacy on behalf of a plan to spur job creation—realizing that he could shift the public agenda, even if he could not persuade congressional Republicans to vote for his proposals. In general, on domestic policy Obama can articulate, very powerfully, why government must help individuals and businesses prepare to work and create a stronger national economy. He is also in charge of foreign policy, a sphere full of risks but also clear rewards for any president. The approval "bump" in polling following the Obama administration's successful raid into Pakistan to kill Osama bin Laden may have been brief; but that major military coup reinforced an underlying sense that Obama can be a strong leader.

Beyond using the bully pulpit and exercising leadership in military and foreign affairs, Obama can also set parameters for deals with Congress on the budget and other fundamentals. True, he cannot write the budgets. But the Senate remains in Democratic hands, and stops many unacceptable bills from even reaching Obama's desk. The White House can signal that it will veto bills that outright repeal critical elements of Obama's reform programs. Furthermore, Obama's Cabinet officers will keep finding ways to move forward with implementation amid hearings and budgetary roadblocks. Cabinet officers such as Kathleen Sebelius at Health and Human Services have considerable ability to move resources around to meet top priorities, even when Congress tries to micromanage.

Chances are that the Obama administration will succeed in moving forward in the key areas where breakthrough legislation occurred during 2009 and 2010, as well as in areas where action occurs primarily by administrative means. In the critical area of comprehensive health reform, for example, Larry Jacobs and I argued in our book *Health Reform and American Politics* that the Affordable Care Act of 2010 will survive as a framework, and many of its key regulations and subsidies will persist.[78] Even if public opinion on health reform remains divided overall, most citizens like many of the specifics in the Affordable Care Act, and particular popular provisions are steadily taking hold.[79] The Democratic advantage on health care is growing now that Republicans have signaled their plan to privatize Medicare and radically reduce future federal spending on health care for the elderly. By large margins, Americans disapprove of the Ryan plan to turn Medicare into vouchers of diminishing value to buy private health insurance.[80] In all areas of health care, President Obama will be able to highlight benefits that Republicans are trying to take away through repeal, de-funding, or radical restructurings of long-standing federal programs. Even business interests may split on some of the GOP proposals for fundamental cutbacks or restructurings. Sectors of business that originally opposed Affordable Care, revisions in educational loans, or other Obama reforms may decide that they would rather push for adjustments than support continuing battles over repeal or wholesale revision.

THE AMERICAN PROSPECT

Moving beyond contemplation of what may happen to legislation or rule shifts that Obama and his congressional supporters pushed onto the books during 2009 and 2010, we must ponder what will happen to the United States if future election cycles reinforce gridlock, or if the political initiative decisively shifts toward highly ideological, antigovernment politicians. Whatever one may think of the reforms the early Obama administration pursued, the president asked Congress and the country to grapple with truly pressing challenges—economic renewal, environmental degradation, declining educational performance and uneven access to postsecondary institutions, a broken immigration system, and a costly but inefficient health care system, as well as other festering dilemmas. All these are very real problems not likely to go away. Many are epochal challenges that affect America's international competitiveness as well as its ability to expand the economy and marshal all available human talents. What does it mean if the U.S. federal government is further weakened in its capacity to deal with major issues, both politically and administratively?

This question becomes all the more pointed when growing federal deficits are brought into the picture—in a polity where powerful partisan and movement forces prefer rhetorically vapid proposals instead of genuine steps to address the most expensive items in the government's portfolio of existing commitments. D.C. Republicans and their allies rigidly oppose tax increases even if they are part of a grand bargain that might include trims of entitlements as well as reforms of the tax code. The unresolved challenges of immigration, energy and climate change, and revenue cannot be wished away, yet the political forces now at work are contradictory and toxic, especially in the midst of an economic and employment slowdown that neither the Obama administration nor congressional Republicans are addressing effectively.

The looming political dangers for both major parties are obvious. Hurt by a slow and incomplete economic recovery, Democrats may lose the presidency and the Senate in 2012. But how will Republicans fare with the American public if Republican governors increase unemployment in their states by slashing public infrastructure projects and throwing teachers, police, and firefighters out of work or shrinking their paychecks? By the middle of 2011, Republican governors and legislators who took such steps became very unpopular with voters.[81] And what will happen to the Republican Party's identity as it becomes solidly identified with the very unpopular Ryan plan to gut Medicare for future generations of grandmothers and grandfathers? Or if House Republicans focus on contentious social issues rather than the economy and continue to threaten government shutdowns? Public disgust with both major parties could continue to grow.

Some analysts speculate that the doors will open to independent or third-party candidacies. But the institutional obstacles in America's federated electoral system are great, likely to prevent sustained third-party capacity from emerging on a national scale. Lone-wolf independents (like Ross Perot in 1992 and 1996) are more likely; but most serve as little more than electoral spoilers, and should an independent actually win major office, he or she would find it hard to make government work. Pounding the desk and shouting will not be sufficient. More likely will be a continual roiling, as American voters throw first one and then another party incumbent out of office. Divided governance amid continual roiling may be very likely for America for the balance of this decade. And this outcome could lead to a further degradation of public capacities, not to mention deepening voter disillusionment.

Perhaps these discouraging scenarios will not come to pass. There is some reason to believe, for example, that the Tea Party has reached a plateau as a mass phenomenon. Its adherents are elderly, after all, and younger people are not joining. Establishment forces find the grassroots activists less and less useful—both Fox News and the Republican Party will do all they can to take the spotlight away from grassroots Tea Partiers during 2012. They see that the general American public is turning sour on Tea Party leaders and ideas, as people see more of what they are saying and demanding.[82] Tea Party ideas tend to be shrill, a bit paranoid, and highly abstract. As specifics about public budgets and taxes come into view, even many grassroots Tea Partiers, and certainly many other Americans, tend to lose enthusiasm for the radical steps that highly ideological right-wing elites favor. During 2012, with the presidency at stake, the Republican Party as a whole will try to keep Tea Partiers aroused enough to vote for whomever it puts up against Obama, while at the same time fudging any radical policy steps that might unfold if Republicans win both the presidency and Congress. In tone at least, Republicans will try to seem more moderate during the general election period of 2012.

President Obama, moreover, is never to be underestimated. He can score on defense, to use a football metaphor. He may be able to nudge GOP leaders in Washington into one compromise after another on the budget and taxes, while maintaining the many second New Deal reforms he and his party achieved with so much difficulty during 2009 and 2010. Where Republicans will not compromise, the president can call them out for their intransigence and draw clear contrasts on issues of taxation, job creation, and public spending where he, not the GOP, is on the side of popular opinion.

Looking back at the first New Deal, it is telling that Franklin Delano Roosevelt got a lot of his early proposals enacted with lightning speed during 1933 and 1934—but his first efforts did *not* prove durable or economically sufficient. The Supreme Court invalidated much of his initial National Recovery Act, and the economy struggled to revive—and eventually went into another tailspin after Roosevelt, in his second term, cut back federal spending under conservative pressure. Many of the enduring legislative reforms of the New Deal—the ones that laid the basis for postwar prosperity in a middle-class society—came from progressive movements and congressional liberals pressing forward somewhat independently from FDR, or took force during World War II.

History is certainly not simply repeating itself. The phases and dynamics of the Obama reformist presidency have been and will remain different, above all because of the interplay of different political and institutional dynamics with a deep economic crisis whose arrival coincided with the start of the Obama presidency. But the past should remind us that the entire unfolding of politics in a period of crisis does not happen at once, and surprising turns are possible. Popular protests can happen on the left as well as the right, as the Occupy Wall Street outbursts have demonstrated. And in Washington, President Obama has time through 2012, and perhaps four more years after that, to cement and propel his renovations of U.S. policies.

Even if Obama is relegated to one term, the big legislative accomplishments of the first two years will define political struggles after 2013—yes, a triumphant GOP may fully repeal or effectively gut Affordable Care before it fully takes effect in 2014, but what then? Contemporary Republicans have gone all-in to say "no" to everything Obama and the Democrats try to do to address pressing national problems. But those problems remain, and the American citizenry as a whole is not enamored of the GOP answers to all issues: cut taxes on the very rich and reduce protections for all other Americans. Ironically, an across-the-board Republican triumph in 2012 could quickly propel changes within the Democratic Party and a return of Democrats to office in states and at the national level in 2014 and 2016.

The expectations for a smoothly executed, politically self-reinforcing second New Deal that accompanied Barack Obama's election and inauguration in 2009—those expectations are long gone. Nothing can gainsay the fact that Obama's White House fell far short of quickly leading the nation to a confident economic recovery—and it is even more obvious that Obama's early policy efforts did not pay immediate political dividends for the Democratic Party, or reinforce the organizational capacities of allies such as the organized labor movement. Indeed, one can argue, as I have here, that the coincidence of a financially induced economic crisis with cautious yet energetic policy reforms not easily understood by ordinary citizens did a lot to fuel huge Democratic losses in 2010 and the Tea Party backlash. That backlash, in turn, not only set back Obama and Democrats, but has pushed the Republican Party toward truly extreme policy stands on taxes and public budgets—and away from any sense of a positive role for the federal government in promoting general welfare.

The Republican Party and the nation as a whole have traveled light years away from Dwight Eisenhower's and

Richard Nixon's acceptance of the welfare state, and even very far from Ronald Reagan's willingness to combine tax increases with spending cuts to manage the federal budget. We Americans cannot yet know where such an extreme Republican Party, determined to slash and bash at government, to repeal or eviscerate the foundations set by the first New Deal and the Great Society, is going to take our democracy. We have entered uncharted waters—and we might conclude that Barack Obama and the Democratic Party of 2008 to 2010 did just enough stirring to break open a hornets' nest, yet not enough to contain the threat.

Politicians alone are not really steering the car as we careen toward what will be yet another nationally pivotal election in 2012. Much depends on whether the current economic recovery continues and gathers sufficient strength to put more Americans to work. Jobs and growth are what Americans care about. Reforms in revenues, health care, energy policy, education, labor relations, and immigration—all are inextricably tied up with economic policy and national economic trends. U.S. political and governing capacity may also hinge on economic effectiveness because a revived economy and less rancorous politics will ease tough decisions about taxes and expenditures on national priorities for the future. U.S. democracy and governance can go in very different directions, depending on our near-term economic fortunes and the mobilization of citizens and leaders to shape political outcomes—including the next round of pivotal elections in 2012.

The last few years have been anything but dull for those of us who study U.S. politics and public policy and care about American democracy in all of its dimensions—from deals in the halls of Congress to protests in the streets and citizen engagement in local meeting halls. There is plenty to investigate and think through. And the riveting moments are not over. Even more turnarounds may be yet to come in American politics, with its constant surprises. We will just have to wait and see—and be mindful that we live, study, and debate in unusually unsettled and consequential times.

2

A NEW DEAL FANTASY MEETS
OLD POLITICAL REALITIES

Larry M. Bartels

Relief there has been, but little more than enough to keep the population fed, clothed and warmed. Recovery there has been, but only to a point still well below the pre-depression level. The great problems of the country are still hardly touched.

—The Editors of *The Economist, The New Deal: An Analysis and Appraisal* (1937)[1]

PROFESSOR SKOCPOL'S ESSAY PROVIDES BOTH AN IN-sightful account of the first two years of the Obama presidency and a wide-ranging rumination on the current state and future prospects of American democracy. It is a very impressive example of authoritative, timely, and politically relevant political science—and a very worthy companion to her edited volume with Lawrence Jacobs, *Reaching for a New Deal,* which addresses some of the same themes at greater length.[2] My remarks will underscore and elaborate aspects of Skocpol's analysis rather than challenging it in any fundamental way.

I do differ with Skocpol's framing of her analysis, which seems to me to give excessive credence to a simplistic view of the "transformative" potential of the Obama presidency. Given that framing, it is hardly surprising that her discussion of what she calls "Obama's Halfway New Deal" mostly portrays it as half empty rather than half full—"just enough to provoke powerful enemies, while leaving . . . political friends, actual and potential, disappointed and mystified," as she puts it. My own inclination is to see the same political history as a good deal less mystifying and, by any realistic standard, a good deal less disappointing.

Skocpol begins her account with a political fantasy: Barack Obama entering the White House as the reincarnation of Franklin Roosevelt, having already transformed American electoral politics by forging a new Democratic majority in the 2008 election and poised to transform American public policy by forging a "new New Deal."

Whose fantasy is this, exactly? The picture of Obama as FDR and the proclamation of "The *New* New Deal" appeared on the cover of *Time* magazine shortly after the 2008 election.[3] Skocpol acknowledges that *Time*'s take "might have been a bit over the top," but immediately adds that "many pundits at the time agreed" with it. She goes on to say that the 2008 election "seemed to open the door to more than incremental shifts in U.S. policy and politics" in "a number of ways" that she enumerates in some detail.

What Skocpol does not say, but should, is that the comparison between Obama and FDR was always highly fanciful. The 2008 election did not mark the "rebirth of American liberalism," as Peter Beinart wrote in *Time*'s cover story; nor did Obama have "an excellent chance" to "establish a Democratic majority that dominates U.S. politics for a generation."[4] Nevertheless, Beinart's piece was fairly representative of a lively genre of triumphal progressive punditry produced in the immediate wake of Obama's election. While Beinart proclaimed "The New Liberal Order," John Judis in the *New*

Republic announced that the 2008 election was "the culmination of a Democratic realignment that began in the 1990s."[5] Even before the election, Robert Kuttner had published a book premised on the equally wishful notion that Obama was poised to be "a transformative progressive president."[6]

For the coterie of liberal pundits who thought they saw a fundamental political realignment with a cherry of progressive transformation on top, the reality of the Obama administration was bound to be disappointing. But political scientists should know better, and indeed most *did* know better. Thus, I find myself wishing that Skocpol—a supremely accomplished scholar with enormous credibility in both camps—had brought some straightforward political science to bear on the naïveté of liberal political commentators rather than seeming to take their mystified disappointment so much to heart.

Within days of Obama's victory, scholars of American voting behavior were pointing out that, from an electoral standpoint, nothing very unusual had happened. The aggregate national vote swing from 2004 to 2008 was no larger than has been typical in presidential elections over the past thirty years—and only about one-third as large as the electoral tide that swept FDR into the White House in 1932. The outcome could be well accounted for by the usual "fundamentals" emphasized in scholarly analyses of election outcomes. Nor was there a greater-than-usual amount of "realigning" of specific states or regions or a greater-than-usual erosion of previous partisan voting patterns. As one expert put it at the time, pundit-talk of realignment was "much-overblown."[7]

It hardly seems coincidental that some of the same liberal pundits who grossly misread the significance of the 2008 election reappear in Skocpol's survey of Obama's "disappointed and mystified" friends. For example, in August 2010, John Judis published a much-talked-about analysis of Obama's "Unnecessary Fall."[8] Why unnecessary? Presumably because Judis had explained less than twenty months earlier that "liberal views have re-emerged . . . with a vengeance, and can be expected to shift further leftward—especially on economic questions—in the face of coming recession. . . . If Obama and the Democrats in Congress act boldly, they can not only arrest the downturn, but also lay the basis for an enduring majority."[9] Didn't they get the memo?

Robert Kuttner's high regard for Obama's capacity to be "a transformative progressive president" was equally quick to shift to disillusionment. Halfway through the president's term, Kuttner published a review essay organized around the thesis that the Obama presidency was "shaping up as one of American history's epic missed moments." Was he really regretting "Obama's failure to rise to the challenge that history dealt him," or Obama's failure to live up to Kuttner's own unrealistic expectations?[10]

Fortunately, while Skocpol begins her account with the simplistic image of Obama as FDR, she proceeds to offer a nuanced and sophisticated comparison between contemporary American politics and the New Deal era—not on the presumption "that Obama's early presidency is similar to the original New Deal," but as a way "to *highlight contrasts* between two periods of reformist Democratic politics amid deep economic crises."

One important difference highlighted by Skocpol is that "Roosevelt took office several years into the Great Depression, when the U.S. economy was at a nadir," whereas "Obama took office amid a sudden financial seizure that was just beginning to push the national economy into a downturn of as-yet-undetermined proportions." This difference in timing seems sufficient in itself to cast considerable doubt on the notion that Obama could have presided over "a Franklin D. Roosevelt moment" of the sort expected by Kuttner.[11]

In the six months following the collapse of Lehman Brothers in September 2008, a series of policy responses improvised by the Federal Reserve, the Treasury Department, and the Obama White House stabilized the financial system and stimulated the economy, averting what might have been a catastrophic meltdown. A bipartisan analysis of "How the Great Recession Was Brought to an End" estimated that this "stunning range of initiatives" boosted real GDP by 4.9 percent in 2009 and 6.6 percent in 2010.[12] Real disposable income per capita still fell by 6 percent between the second quarter of 2008 and the fourth quarter of 2009—but that was less than one-fourth of the percentage drop during the Great Depression, and most of it occurred before Obama took office. Meanwhile, the S&P 500 stock index rose almost 60 percent during Obama's first two years in the White House, regaining most of the ground it had lost from its peak in 2007 to the end of the Bush administration.

Of course, the millions of Americans who had lost their jobs or their homes were unlikely to be cheered by the fact that things might have been much worse. However, from a political perspective, what may be most remarkable about the Great Recession is the starkness of the division between casualties and noncombatants. While victims of the economic crisis in Greece, France, and Britain took to the streets, America's millions of unemployed and foreclosed were virtually invisible. A majority of respondents in a 2010 survey said that they *did not know* "anyone who has had their home foreclosed or fallen behind in their mortgage payments in the past year."[13] For most Americans, a few months of genuine panic fairly quickly faded into the more familiar economic strain of recession and slow recovery.

Skocpol also rightly emphasizes differences in the composition and procedures of Congress between the 1930s and the present. Whereas "Roosevelt enjoyed bipartisan support for recovery efforts launched at an economic nadir," Obama faced "the very early crystallization of GOP opposition" to his policy agenda. With the filibuster having evolved "from an extraordinary expression into a routine obstructive tactic . . . legislative action was ever-precarious in the Senate."

Indeed, the basic legislative dynamics of the Obama administration reflect with remarkable precision the logic of Keith Krehbiel's influential "pivotal politics" model.[14] In a world where almost every significant piece of legislation is subject to a Senate filibuster, the simple fact is that a Democratic president can only be as liberal as the sixtieth-most-liberal senator allows him to be. Exactly what that means in the context of any specific instance of policymaking is seldom entirely clear. Nevertheless, Krehbiel's model focuses attention where it belongs, on the handful of pivotal senators who would or would not provide the crucial votes in support of Obama's key legislative initiatives.

The most striking aspect of the major legislative battles of 2009 and 2010 is how, time after time, Obama and his allies in Congress pushed precisely to the limit of "pivotal politics." Economic stimulus, health care reform, and financial regulation all passed the Senate with exactly sixty votes. In each case, pivotal senators extracted significant concessions in exchange for their support, resulting in more modest policy changes than would otherwise have occurred. Critics who demanded more—the disappointed and mystified political friends of Skocpol's account—either misunderstood the basic parameters of American lawmaking or vastly overestimated the power of progressive rhetoric to alter the fundamental preferences of some decidedly unprogressive politicians.

Only a few weeks after President Obama's inauguration, Congress passed a massive $787 billion stimulus bill, the American Recovery and Reinvestment Act. The legislation cleared the Senate only when Ohio Democrat Sherrod Brown returned from his mother's funeral to cast the pivotal sixtieth vote.[15] According to the *New York Times,* "Many Democrats would have preferred a larger bill, but agreed to pare back, including cuts to favored education and health programs, to win three crucial Republican votes in the Senate."[16]

Skocpol notes that the prospect of a larger stimulus "did not seem realistic to the fledgling Obama White House, which felt it had to stay under a trillion to win congressional support. Perhaps naïvely, Obama also tried to woo congressional Republicans with substantial up-front tax cuts . . . [but] got fewer than a handful of GOP votes in return for his gestures." She adds that Obama's strategy was "understandable for a brand-new president . . . who had just promised the electorate he would change the political tone in Washington." Finally, in half a sentence, she acknowledges that "it is not clear that any larger package could have gotten through Congress." But if that is true—if a "fledgling," "perhaps naïve" president won as big a stimulus as he could have won given the configuration of preferences in Congress—then "expert postmortems" that "bemoaned the insufficient size of the stimulus package" are nothing more than idle Monday morning quarterbacking.

The landmark health care reform bill likewise passed with exactly sixty votes in the Senate. In this case the quest for sixty votes was much longer, more public, and more politically debilitating than for the stimulus bill. To progressives, the most frustrating phase of the process was the summer-long courtship of key Republicans by Max Baucus, the moderate Democrat who chaired the powerful Senate Finance Committee. Baucus failed to bring along the senior Republican on his committee, Charles Grassley, but did secure the vote of pivotal Republican Olympia Snowe and those of fellow-moderate Democrats Kent Conrad and Bill Nelson.[17]

Having given Senator Baucus a free hand to attempt consensus building among key moderates, President Obama then pivoted to his left, giving Senate majority leader Harry Reid an equally free hand to try to push the bill in a more progressive direction by reinstating the "public option" jettisoned by Baucus. Having spurned Snowe's support, Reid would need every Democratic vote as well as that of cranky ex-Democrat Joseph Lieberman. After two months of high-profile negotiations finally seemed to produce an agreement, Lieberman reversed course, threatening on national television to block the bill unless the public option was deleted. Reid and the White House reluctantly agreed, and after another week of horse trading with moderate Ben Nelson over special favors for Nebraska—and a futile threat of revolt by restive progressives—the Senate bill advanced on a 60–40 party-line cloture vote, finally passing with the same sixty votes in a dramatic Christmas Eve session.[18]

In retrospect, the long, drawn-out attempt to revive the public option was a costly political error, lodging health care at the top of the legislative agenda for additional precious months. That error goes unremarked by Obama's liberal critics because it does not fit their narrative of "political timidity" and "a blind faith in bipartisanship," as Judis put it.[19]

Nevertheless, the collapse of Reid's effort to cobble together sixty votes for the public option left the final legislation not far from where it had been in October. When a special election in January brought a stunning end to the Democrats' brief "filibuster-proof" Senate majority, even that bridge less far came close to collapsing. Only in April, through the ramshackle mechanism of reconciliation—and reportedly with some timely spine-stiffening from House Speaker Nancy Pelosi—did the Affordable Care Act become law.[20]

It is not hard to see why all of this might be disappointing and mystifying to anyone observing the long, messy process of health care reform. However, it is harder to see why progressive observers should have been either mystified or disappointed by the *outcome* of that process. In a front-page article in the *New York Times,* David Leonhardt described the Affordable Care Act as "the most sweeping piece of federal legislation since Medicare was passed in 1965," adding that its progressive financing provisions also made it "the federal government's biggest attack on economic inequality since inequality began rising more than three decades ago."[21]

It was clear from the outset—or should have been—that no health care reform bill would pass without support from the likes of Baucus, Conrad, Lieberman, and Nelson, if not Grassley and Snowe. Absent some magical shift in the views of these pivotal senators, how was the president supposed to achieve his policy goals, if not through compromise? The answer, according to disappointed liberals, lies in the power of a "transformative" presidency. According to Kuttner, a "static view of the array of political forces lets Obama off the hook too easily, because it ignores the unique role—or absence—of presidential leadership." Through a "potent combination of insider leadership, mobilization of public opinion, and alliance with social movements on the ground," Obama should have been able to engineer policy changes comparable in magnitude to those produced by Roosevelt and Lyndon Johnson.[22] It is a convenient supposition, but Kuttner offers no evidence for his conviction that "presidential leadership" and "mobilization of public opinion" could have transformed a hard-fought compromise into a progressive triumph.

Skocpol notes that "GOP congressional leaders decided from the start of Obama's presidency to pursue a strategy of all-out opposition—a strategy they could hope to implement, given that smaller, more conservative congressional flocks were easier to manage." This is certainly right as far as it goes, but it seems to me to underplay both the difficulty and the limited success of Senate minority leader Mitch McConnell's efforts to "manage" the handful of moderate Republican senators whose cooperation was crucial to the president's legislative agenda. Obama and Reid needed three Republican votes for the economic stimulus bill, and they got them. Olympia Snowe bucked the Republican leadership by supporting the Baucus health care bill in committee before Reid decided to pursue a pure party-line strategy on the floor. Snowe and Susan Collins both crossed over to support the White House's plan for financial regulation—and when a purist gesture by Wisconsin Democrat Russ Feingold left supporters still one vote short, additional concessions produced a third Republican vote from newcomer Scott Brown.[23]

Of course, other major policy initiatives—most notably in the areas of energy and immigration—*were* stymied by opposition in the Senate. But as Skocpol notes, the opponents in both these cases included more than a few Democrats intensely cross-pressured by local interests. Thus, the Republicans' "strategy of all-out opposition" was hardly crucial in accounting for the absence of policy change. In these domains, an even larger dose of transformational leadership pixie dust would have been required to achieve ambitious progressive policy outcomes.

Pivotal politicians on both sides of the aisle were well aware that the public's taste for ambitious policy initiatives was limited. Many supported those initiatives nonetheless. The result was a string of significant legislative successes, but with a significant political price tag attached. For Democrats in Congress, the bill came due in the 2010 midterm election. A vote-by-vote analysis by Eric McGhee suggests that supporting the Affordable Care Act cost a typical Democrat 4.5 percent of the vote in 2010; supporting the ambitious cap-and-trade energy bill cost an additional 2.1 percent. For both these votes, the estimated electoral costs were even greater for Democrats in swing districts. A simulation based on these estimates suggested that if every vulnerable Democrat had refrained from voting for just these two bills the party would have lost twenty-four fewer seats, bringing the election outcome into close agreement with forecasts based primarily on the state of the economy.[24]

Congressional Democrats also seem to have been punished in 2010 for having supported the Obama stimulus plan. However, in this instance the direct electoral penalty was probably more than offset by the indirect electoral benefit of additional economic growth.[25] Of course, an even more ambitious stimulus—had it been feasible—might have produced even more economic growth, and thus even more electoral benefit, in 2010 and 2012. Nevertheless, in purely electoral terms the stimulus very likely "paid" for itself, notwithstanding widespread public skepticism about its economic effectiveness. That was certainly not true of health care reform, since, as Skocpol notes, most of the concrete benefits stemming from the Affordable Care Act were both distant and uncertain. And the cap-and-trade vote was even less productive from a political standpoint, since the reform effort subsequently collapsed in the Senate without producing any actual policy benefits for anyone.

Skocpol seems to attribute the "endless political controversy and electoral blowback" of 2009 and 2010 primarily to the "incomprehension and anxiety of everyday Americans" faced with bewildering policy debates, and to "a veritable explosion of political pushback" from "business interests and many wealthy conservatives." However, like Kuttner, she also blames "Obama's failure to engage more consistently in high-profile public leadership," calling it "democratic political malpractice." Although the president "traveled the country highlighting economic initiatives and progress in selected areas," she argues, "such efforts lacked the galvanizing, agenda-setting effect of a major speech or sustained national communications strategy; and their fragmented focus inherently restricted the White House's ability to present a coherent economic plan."

This argument seems to me to put undue stock in the power of the "bully pulpit" to sway public opinion—a mythical power that has mostly failed to withstand systematic scholarly scrutiny.[26] It also fails to account for the fact that the most costly "electoral blowback" against the president's congressional allies in 2010 seems not to have come in reaction to his misunderstood economic plan, but in reaction to his ambitious health care reform—the very policy area in which, by Skocpol's account, "Obama gave major speeches and orchestrated theatrically effective issue forums at key intervals during 2009 and early 2010, displaying presidential leadership and offering framings that proved influential beyond as well as within the Beltway." If this was an example of the "bully pulpit" in action, it is hardly surprising that Democrats in Congress were not eager to stake their careers on further experiments in progressive "presidential leadership."

In the wake of the Republicans' big midterm election gains, Skocpol suggests that "the time for major legislative breakthroughs has come and gone—at least until after a possible Obama reelection in 2012." But imagine that Democrats had lost no seats at all in 2010. What "legislative breakthroughs" would then have been forthcoming in 2011 and 2012? I can't think of any. For all the blood, sweat, and tears it took to grind out narrow, ugly legislative victories on the economic stimulus, health care reform, and financial regulation, *that was the easy stuff.*

Unlike many less sophisticated progressives, Skocpol clearly recognizes the magnitude of Obama's policy successes during his first two years in office. "Given all of the difficulties the president and Democrats faced in 2009 and 2010," she says, "if we are just toting up legislative and regulatory accomplishments, the bills passed and decisions issued, Obama's ambitious agenda for policy change progressed quite remarkably—to institute comprehensive health reform, reform higher education loans, tighten regulation of financial institutions, and tweak many other realms of law and regulation. A new New Deal of sorts *was* successfully launched by President Obama and congressional Democrats in 2009 and 2010."

Obama's problem, in Skocpol's view, has had less to do with *policies* than with *politics*. "A new New Deal of sorts *was* successfully launched by President Obama and congressional Democrats in 2009 and 2010. But much of what happened was either invisible or ominously incomprehensible to the majority of American citizens." She contrasts this state of affairs with the New Deal era: "Back in the 1930s, American citizens could see that big, new things were being proposed and debated in Washington."

I wonder whether the policy changes championed by Roosevelt were really so much more visible and comprehensible— or, for that matter, more popular—than those pursued by Obama. Sociologists Katherine Newman and Elisabeth Jacobs have revisited the New Deal era and found a variety of striking parallels with the present.

For one thing, FDR, like Obama, had plenty of disappointed and mystified friends. Newman and Jacobs wrote, "Though we remember Roosevelt today as the man who did more for the poor and dispossessed than any president before, and arguably anyone since, in his own day leftists and labor liberals often complained that Roosevelt's actions were too little, too late, and too tepid."[27]

FDR also had plenty of success in provoking enemies. Political polarization in the 1930s was less strictly along partisan lines than it is today, but it would be a mistake to jump to the conclusion that it was any less severe. For example, in a Gallup survey conducted in 1936, at the height of FDR's popularity, Americans were asked, "Do you believe the acts and policies of the Roosevelt Administration may lead to dictatorship?" A remarkable 45 percent of the respondents— and 83 percent of Republicans—said yes.[28]

Some of the angry letters to the president quoted by New-man and Jacobs sound eerily similar to the rhetoric of today's right-wing Republicans. "The forgotten man," one constituent wrote, alluding to one of FDR's main campaign themes, "is NOT the shiftless, indifferent individual, who believes the world owe [*sic*] him a living (and is now getting it). The forgotten man in your administration is the thrifty middle class who have striven to make this country worth living in—whom you are striving to wipe out of existence."[29]

Moreover, the political disputes of the 1930s dredged up many of the same cultural and racial tensions evident in contemporary Tea Party politics. One of Roosevelt's unhappy constituents wrote,

> Do you recall the fate of that great "purger" of the French Revolution, Robespierre? Well, the voters of these United States still possess the right to change the complexion of Congress every two years and can politically "purge" most effectively. We mean to do this without the aid of bought Negro relievers, WPA-ers, subsidized non-producers, pampered Alien and Labor Union hangers-on, or that misguided coterie surrounding you who have so amiably and so senselessly squandered our billions. We prefer to link up with the yearly increment of American-born new voters who will remember their heritage and keep it clean.[30]

Skocpol notes in closing that "U.S. democracy and governance can go in very different directions, depending on our near-term economic fortunes and the mobilization of citizens and leaders to shape political outcomes—including the next round of pivotal elections in 2012." I certainly agree; but I submit that this, too, is a long-standing political reality rather than a special feature of the "interesting and consequential times" in which we find ourselves now. And here, too, the New Deal era seems to me to provide a very informative reference point.

In the conventional understanding of the electoral politics of the 1930s, the forging of a durable new partisan alignment hinged crucially on popular responses to the policies and personality of FDR. V. O. Key Jr. claimed that the Democratic landslide of 1936 had "a special significance. . . . The result could only be interpreted as a popular ratification of the broad features of new public policy." James Sundquist wrote that voters were "attracted by the Democratic program and the Rooseveltian personality and leadership." Even the authors of *The American Voter,* who famously downplayed the importance of ideology for most voters most of the time, attributed the "profound realignment of party strength" in the 1930s to "the program of welfare legislation of the New Deal and the extraordinary personality of its major exponent, Franklin D. Roosevelt."[31]

In contrast to this conventional view, I think there is good reason to believe that Roosevelt's political fate was just as dependent as Obama's has been and will be on "near-term economic fortunes." My colleague Christopher Achen and I have shown that Roosevelt's 1936 landslide was heavily concentrated in states with very high income growth rates over the course of the election year. (Even in the midst of economic distress, voters were highly myopic; thus, income growth in 1934 and 1935 had no discernible impact in 1936.) Our analysis suggests that, if the recession of 1938 had happened to occur two years earlier, FDR would probably have been a one-term president.[32] In that case, the New Deal era would have been just as evanescent as the "New Liberal Order" proclaimed by Peter Beinart in 2008.

Moreover, there is surprisingly little trace in the electoral politics of the 1930s of any coherent ideological realignment of the sort taken for granted by many subsequent scholars. In the United States, for example, states with large numbers of poor, black, foreign-born, or rural people were not significantly more supportive of Roosevelt or of Democratic congressional candidates, once we allow for differences in election-year income growth. And in the other democracies of the world, voters in the depths of the Great Depression showed a notable willingness to replace incumbents of every ideological stripe with an equally diverse range of alternatives, including conservatives, socialists, Irish nationalists, Nazis, and (in the Canadian prairie province of Alberta) a radio preacher running on a platform of distributing free money.[33] As David Mayhew put it in his masterful debunking of the scholarly literature on American party realignments, "academics have tended to dismiss campaign slogans of the past like 'the full dinner pail' and 'a chicken in every pot' on the grounds that something deeper must have been going on in these elections. But perhaps it wasn't."[34]

If even the New Deal era does not live up to our heroic expectations for "transformational" politics, what chance has Obama? Perhaps it is finally time to let go of that fantasy, and to assess the successes and failures of our own era in the light of enduring political realities.

> If the criterion be Utopian, the achievements of the New Deal appear to be small. . . . [But i]f the New Deal be compared, not with the absolute standards of Utopia,

but with the achievements of other Governments, the former adverse judgement must be modified. If it be compared with either the performance or the promise of its rivals, it comes out well. If its achievements be compared with the situation which confronted it in March, 1933, it is a striking success.

—The Editors of *The Economist, The New Deal: An Analysis and Appraisal* (1937)[35]

3

OBAMA'S PROBLEM: MISREADING THE MANDATE

Mickey Edwards

PROFESSOR SKOCPOL HAS DONE HER USUAL SUPERB job in evaluating the successes and failures of the Obama administration to this point and in looking critically at the current state of American politics. It is my goal merely to suggest some additional thoughts that may help expand the conversation.

To consider why things might have gone wrong during the first years of the Obama presidency—Professor Skocpol's assumption is that things *did* go wrong—it might help to take a brief look at what happened to another presidency that began nearly thirty years earlier and found itself after two years in much the same place President Obama is today.

In 1980, Ronald Reagan carried forty-four states and won the electoral college 489 to 49. *One* possible explanation for such an impressive outcome—the explanation favored by Mr. Reagan's supporters, myself among them—was that the American people had rebelled against a government that they believed had become too big, too expensive, too intrusive. *In this scenario,* Reagan's election was a mandate to move the country in a more conservative direction, with fewer government programs, lower taxes, less regulation, and in the areas of foreign and defense policy a much more muscular confrontation with the Soviet Union.

The *other* possibility was that voters had simply tired of Jimmy Carter; that they considered him unsuited for the office he occupied; that they were tired of his woeful countenance, that they were tired of what they perceived to be a pervasive ineptitude whether dealing with Iran or inflation. They wanted him gone and Ronald Reagan was the only serious alternative. Besides, with a third candidate, John Anderson, a much more liberal Republican, on the ballot, Reagan, the only conservative among the three, received less than 51 percent of the popular vote. And against an opponent who first had to fend off a serious challenge in his own party. *Hardly* an overwhelming landslide.

There was some validity to both interpretations—by the end of November 1984, there had been 100 separate state elections for president in which Ronald Reagan was a candidate—two in each of the fifty states—and Reagan had won 93 of those 100 elections. But while he enjoyed an occasional working majority in Congress during his first two years, voters punished his party in the midterm elections after he had been in office for just two years. And while he later regained much of his lost popularity and was reelected overwhelmingly, he was never again given a Congress whose support he could count on.

Reagan's supporters, myself among them, misread those 1980 election results: we believed the rest of the country saw the election as we did, saw Reagan as we did, and had given us a mandate. We ignored the possibility that our victory had been due in large part to disaffection with Jimmy Carter and we set about to create a new—and, we thought, desired—conservative America.

Professor Skocpol believes—I am oversimplifying her argument here—that President Obama's difficulties in 2009 and 2010 were due either to outside forces—the Tea Party, Fox News, right-wing millionaires, an electorate that could not understand complicated questions—or to the president's failure to better explain his actions. Those are not invalid points and each of them has some merit. But her analysis leaves out one important potential variable: that the American people—*including non-millionaires and non–Tea Party members*—*did* understand what the president was proposing and simply disagreed with what he was trying to do. Perhaps President Obama and his supporters did what Ronald Reagan and his supporters did—misread an election's results and assumed they had been given a mandate the voters never intended.

Part of the story of 1980 was a public rejection of Jimmy Carter, who was perceived to be incompetent, and part of the story of 2008 was a rejection of George W. Bush, who was perceived to have a cavalier attitude toward the Constitution and an insufficient reticence about sending young Americans to war. Many Republicans, myself included, supported Barack Obama not because of his policies but because we thought it important to repudiate George W. Bush and because that also required not voting for his preferred successor, who had some problems of his own.

What happens when you believe you have a mandate? You set out to fulfill it and are sometimes surprised to learn that the public you assumed was behind you is instead standing off to the side wondering what it is you think you are doing. I am not suggesting this was the case with most of the people who voted for Barack Obama, but I am suggesting that there may not have been as full-throated a support for his agenda as people in the White House might have imagined. In addition, while Professor Skocpol believes President Obama's initiatives to have been quite modest, they may have appeared more problematic to others than they appeared to her.

There was another problem. Barack Obama made much of his view that there is "not a Red America, not a Blue America, but a United States of America" and of his pledge to work with Republicans in Congress to forge a bipartisan program. I believe the president was sincere. But it was a pledge that overlooked two important facts.

The first was that while we are indeed one country, the Red–Blue divide is not nonexistent; whether it is in the social preferences and religious habits common to different regions of the country or to the different attitudes engendered by urban congestion and open spaces, there are quite serious distinctions between, say, the average Massachusetts voter and the average Oklahoma voter. Having taught at Harvard for eleven years and having served in Congress from Oklahoma for sixteen years before that, I can say with some assurance that the differences in philosophy, in values, in preferences are quite real and quite deeply ingrained—a difference, if I can put it this way, between, on the one hand, those people who own guns and go to church and, on the other, those who see churchgoing gun owners as clinging to guns and religion out of fear of the modern age. We *are* the United States, but we are *also* Red States and Blue States, and that the Obama administration would find serious pushback should have come as no surprise.

When I teach public leadership, I emphasize the need for those who would exercise leadership to be passionate enough to sustain their commitment but at the same time sufficiently dispassionate to be able to objectively assess reality. One possible answer to "what happened" is that the Obama forces, like the Reagan forces thirty years earlier, got caught up in believing that the wisdom of their own preferences was so self-evident that any intelligent person would certainly agree if only one were patient enough in explaining it.

It has often seemed to some on the left that many Americans tend to vote against their own interests, whether the fault is in their lack of ability to comprehend complex questions or in the failure of wiser people to speak slowly enough. But underlying that assessment is an assumption that one's primary interests are always economic whereas many voters may, in fact, put a higher priority on noneconomic factors which are harder to quantify but nonetheless very real parts of the decision-making process.

The second important overlooked fact was this. While some were critical of the president for "letting" the Congress take the lead in drafting legislation, the Constitution places almost every major power of government—the war power, taxing power, spending power, and law-writing power—in the Congress, not in the Executive. What Barack Obama *needed* was a Denny Hastert. When Hastert was Speaker of the House, and a Republican, he considered it his job to serve as legislative floor leader for the Republican president. Nancy Pelosi, to her credit, understood that the principal responsibility for federal policy is in the legislature, and while she supported the president, she made it clear that neither she nor other members of Congress were part of the White House staff. The practical effect of this important and constitutionally correct assumption of responsibility was to limit the ability of the president to seek buy-in from his Republican opponents. The president had won the election, but so had the Democrats in Congress, and as Speaker Pelosi put it, "We won the election; we'll write the bills." She had the votes to prevail and saw no need to compromise away the advantage the voters had conferred.

Professor Skocpol is absolutely correct that Republicans had determined to block the president's initiatives. They did so both out of conviction—a different view of the best course for the nation—and out of a political calculus predicated on the assumption that the nation was more conservative than the president and that being seen as an obstacle to his initiatives was more likely to return power to the Republican Party in the midterms and in 2012. So perhaps any attempt to win Republican support would have failed, but despite what the president might have preferred, there was no serious effort to get up-front bipartisan support for any major part of the Obama agenda.

This leads me to one other factor that limited President Obama's success—an obstacle President Reagan did not have to face. There was certainly partisanship during the Reagan years as well as during the succeeding presidency of George H. W. Bush, and on issues ranging from the first Gulf War to the insurgencies in Central America to the Strategic Defense Initiative and major taxing and spending issues, Republicans tended to support the president and Democrats were generally opposed. But there were also during those presidencies, as in the years before, many issues on which bipartisan majorities could be shaped.

But a poison was seeping into the system. To counter Republican initiatives, which were supported as well by a number of conservative "Boll Weevil" Democrats, the House leadership began to limit opportunities for Republicans to amend the leadership's proposals or offer their own. This had the very unfortunate effect of causing Republicans to turn to a much more partisan leader, Newt Gingrich, under whose leadership Republicans began to see themselves as Republicans first and legislators second. Both parties are now guilty of an escalating and persistent partisan warfare, and whether one believes the fault lies more with Republicans or with Pelosi's declaration that "we won the election, we'll write the bills," for Barack Obama the possibility of cobbling together a program with true bipartisan support had vanished.

Before I conclude with my own assessment of where we go from here, let me turn to Professor Skocpol's discussion of the Tea Party movement. I will devote less attention to this issue than she has because I believe its role and influence have been greatly exaggerated. Tea Party activists support a more limited government and less government spending. That makes them conservative Republicans. And as Professor Skocpol points out, surveys have shown that Tea Party supporters are mostly either Republicans already or Independents who lean Republican. The Tea Party organizations helped conservatives mobilize more vigorous grassroots campaigns than they might have been able to do otherwise and managed to win nominations for some conservative candidates who might not have won otherwise, but intraparty nomination fights are neither new nor uncommon—just ask Joe Lieberman.

In the most captivating example from this past midterm election, Christine O'Donnell defeated Mike Castle for the Republican nomination for the U.S. Senate from Delaware. But in a state with nearly one million people, she won the nomination with only 30,000 votes and then lost badly in November. In Utah, where any Republican who won the nomination was certain to win the general election, Senator

Robert Bennett was denied renomination by a convention at which fewer than one-tenth of one percent of Utah's citizens were in attendance. Most of the so-called Tea Party winners were actually traditional conservative Republicans who came not from the wilderness but through the traditional political system—Marco Rubio had been Speaker of the House in Florida, Kelly Ayotte had been attorney general in New Hampshire, Todd Rokita had been secretary of state in Indiana. Despite the rise of the occasional Rand Paul, the Tea Party mainly helped Republicans who would have been elected anyway. Think not of the Tea Party but of a strengthened base of fiscally conservative Republicans, and it is indeed clear that attempts to hold the line against deep spending cuts will face serious challenges for the next couple of years. Decades ago, conservative Republicans rebelled against the party's leadership and against Presidents Reagan and George H. W. Bush when they proposed to raise taxes or were thought to be insufficiently aggressive in cutting spending. Although some of them are loud and insistent, the so-called Tea Party members of Congress are merely repeating what many others have done before them.

One additional factor in all this, which has not been much remarked upon, is a political system in which parties control access to the general election ballot—thus a mere 30,000 people in Delaware knocking Mike Castle out of the Senate race and one-tenth of one percent of the population of Utah ending Senator Robert Bennett's career. This delegation of power to two private clubs also accounts in part for the difficulties President Obama faced in trying to get bipartisan support, both because parties control redistricting in most states and because party leaders in the House of Representatives control committee assignments, granting desired positions only in exchange for commitments to stick firmly to the party line. That system is responsible to a considerable degree for the fact that on issue after issue Republicans line up in lockstep on one side of the issue and Democrats line up in lockstep on the other. Party unity scores have risen to disturbingly high levels reflecting, in my opinion, a legislature in which members are increasingly reluctant to evaluate proposals on their merits rather than on their partisan provenance. To some extent, it is this acquiescence to a system of political dominance by two private power-seeking clubs that helped undermine President Obama's attempts to enact proposals that would win public support.

Finally, let me take a look at what may lie ahead.

In 1984, Ronald Reagan carried forty-nine of the fifty states. Barack Obama can take some comfort from that fact. Already his numbers are on the way back up. He took his licking in 2010, but he is in a position to regain the political advantage as events push foreign policy forward on the national radar. Many of the liberals who supported Obama in 2008, believing him to be one of them, may not like it, but the president is already reshaping his administration to capture the political center. In addition, as Professor Skocpol has noted, the electorate in 2010 was not the same as it had been in 2008—in the midterm elections voters were more white and more affluent. If all the same people who voted in 2008 had gone to the polls last year, it is possible that the Democratic losses would have been much smaller.

It has been common for the president's supporters to ask why the public so hates this man but even as voters renounced the work of the administration and Congress, the president's own personal popularity remains solid. It may well be that the voters disliked not the man but the agenda. If that is the case, an Obama administration that is more centrist than it could be with a liberal Democratic majority in Congress, coupled with a Republican leadership now under pressure to prove it can get things done rather than merely being a force for obstruction, might make the next two years a bit less difficult for both the president and his party.

4

OBAMA AND THE CHALLENGE
OF SUBMERGED POLICIES

Suzanne Mettler

W HEN BARACK OBAMA WON THE PRESIDENCY IN 2008, his election also ushered in large Democratic majorities in both chambers of Congress, among them Dan Maffei, who would represent the 25th congressional district of New York. The 25th, like many other upstate New York districts, has sent Republicans to Congress for the vast majority of years since before the Civil War—from not long after Alexis de Tocqueville, honored by this book, visited the area on his American sojourn. Over the past several decades, these New York representatives were some of the few remaining Republican moderates in Congress, while the voters who elected them increasingly favored Democratic candidates for the presidency. The 2008 switch in the 25th district, though resulting from gradual, long-term changes in the electorate, was immediately consequential for national policymaking: leading up to major votes in the 111th Congress, Maffei often appeared on Speaker Nancy Pelosi's list of members who could swing either way, and time and again he ultimately cast affirmative votes for President Barack Obama's policy priorities. Most significant, in March 2010 he offered one of the key votes to enable the passage of the reconciliation bill that contained both health care reform and sweeping changes in higher education policy.

In the 2010 midterm election, however, Maffei lost his seat to a Republican contender, one whom local party officials had deemed unthreatening right up to Election Day. Ann Marie Buerkle, who enjoyed Tea Party backing and was endorsed by Sarah Palin as one of the "Mama Grizzlies," possesses views that would have seemed out of step with those of most upstate New Yorkers: she has stated that she considers global warming to be a "myth," she favors abolishing the U.S. Department of Education, and she is committed to repealing health care reform.[1] Yet, in an election year that featured low turnout in the district's more urban areas but long lines at polling places in the suburban and rural areas where Buerkel enjoyed the strongest support, she prevailed.[2]

The electoral changes of fortune in the New York 25th and its implications for Obama's agenda are indicative of the broader patterns in recent American politics that Theda Skocpol has so masterfully portrayed. On the one hand, Obama managed to succeed in enacting much of his agenda during his first two years in office, not least because he had gained large enough majorities of Democrats in Congress to support the passage of major laws. Yet his election and policy agenda also led quickly to a rightward shift in what had already become, in historical perspective, a very conservative Republican Party, and to a GOP resurgence in the midterms that put it back in control of the House, poised to thwart Obama's agenda and the implementation of his policy achievements to date.

Skocpol's comprehensive and trenchant examination of these developments is powerful and mesmerizing. She defies the usual tendency of scholars of American politics to compartmentalize; instead she draws on insights from a wide array of studies as she weaves an analysis encompassing institutional arrangements, patterns of political behavior at the elite and mass levels, and the dynamics of policymaking and policy effects. She also transcends the discipline's penchant for losing track of how time itself matters for politics. She situates her study in historical context, incisively comparing and contrasting the politics of our time with that of the 1930s, and she shows how Obama confronted a particular set of daunting political circumstances—including gaping partisan polarization and a fragmented media environment—that have developed over several decades. She implicitly applies her renowned polity-centered framework—which she developed originally to explain social policy developments in the late nineteenth and early twentieth centuries—and uses it to explain two major puzzles: first, how the American political system happened to permit a reform-minded president to accomplish major policy goals but also why such success failed to reap benefits for his party at election time; and second, how an insurgent mobilization emerged within what seemed to be a devastated Republican Party, and within two years, enabled it to rise like a phoenix from the ashes of the 2008 elections—while shifting its center of gravity in a more conservative direction.

My intent is not to refute this insightful analysis, but rather to focus on a few elements that Skocpol mentions briefly, and to develop them further, utilizing an approach she herself has advanced elsewhere, namely, policy feedback. Here I am referring to how policies created at an earlier time reshape politics—changing state capacities and the social identities, goals, and capabilities of groups—which in turn influences subsequent policymaking. Skocpol notes that Obama faced a different challenge than Roosevelt because rather than starting fresh to create major new national policies, he had to reform a complex set of existing arrangements, ones that had cultivated their own devoted constituencies and stakeholders. I will explore how established policies that have long shaped the political landscape played a crucial role in shaping citizens' awareness and understanding of Obama's reform efforts and the political mobilization that has emerged in response to it. I will argue that Obama's election and his particular policy agenda coalesced to activate these feedback dynamics, with the dual effects of unleashing powerful forces of opposition and generating little by way of support.

The Political Challenges of Reconstituting Governance

Skocpol's analysis begins with a riveting puzzle, which I would phrase like this: How could Obama achieve so much of his policy agenda, and yet fail to reap political benefits from it? This framing might surprise some, particularly many liberals who have been left with the impression that Obama failed to meet his campaign promises, but I consider it to be right on the mark. In fact, in his first year in office, according to *Congressional Quarterly,* Congress acceded to Obama's position on 96.7 percent of votes—a record high since it began to tally such votes in 1953, and higher than the previous record held by Lyndon Johnson.[3] In 2010, Obama's record was not as high but still ranked fourth for presidents in their second year in office, and it included major legislation, not least health care reform—a goal sought in vain by liberals for the better part of a century.[4] The mystery, then, is why, while Obama pursued and met his central objectives, did his supporters—who had packed stadiums and cheered him enthusiastically throughout 2008—seem to recede into the woodwork, while opponents, particularly in the Tea Party movement, grew energized? Why did polling about his major accomplishments—including policies favored by majorities of Americans for decades—yield tepid responses—for instance, with 61 percent saying by the fall of 2010 that they favored the repeal of health care reform?[5] And how could the losses for the president's party on Election Day, though unsurprising in a midterm, be so great in magnitude given his policy achievements?

Many would declare the answer to these questions to be obvious: the worst economic conditions since the Great Depression, with more than two years of nearly 10 percent unemployment. When we compare present circumstances to those of the 1930s, however, the state of the economy alone does not appear to offer a sufficient explanation for Americans' blasé response to major policy accomplishments that reflected broadly shared values. The public voiced its high approval for the Social Security Act of 1935, for example, when the nation was still mired in the Great Depression and when 20 percent of Americans remained jobless, twice the proportion without jobs today. That legislation was also multifaceted and complex, and at the same time it was even more novel for the United States than the Patient Protection and Affordable Care Act of 2010, marking the first major involvement of the U.S. federal government in social provision for people besides veterans and their relatives. In the presidential election of 1936, moreover, Roosevelt himself won by a larger margin than in the previous election, and the Democrats picked up twelve seats.

Skocpol's analysis implicitly refutes the view that the state of the economy single-handedly determines political outcomes; she notes the significance of several political obstacles he faced, not least the sheer scope and complexity of the policy tasks he assumed, the fragmented and partisan media environment, and other factors of his own making, namely, his administration's underwhelming public relations efforts. These observations are all indisputable, but it is Skocpol's comments about the nature of Obama's reformist policy agenda that I find most illuminating of the particular challenges he has confronted, and it is these policy-centered themes on which I will elaborate. In analyzing what she calls "Obama's Halfway New Deal," Skocpol makes two arguments about policy: first, Obama's agenda would not be achieved by creating brand-new policies, but by *re*structuring what already exists; second, because of their particular policy design, many of his accomplishments have been largely invisible to ordinary citizens and thus have gained him little credit. I agree, and would go further, to say that these points are linked, through what I call the *submerged state*.

Political change is always a "*re*construction," to quote Karen Orren and Stephen Skowronek: as they observe, it takes place "on a site, a prior political ground of practices, rules, leaders, and ideas, all of which are up and running."[6] These existing features may present opportunities, but they also pose obstacles that must be surmounted. Certainly Roosevelt confronted a political landscape in the 1930s with its own operating policies and institutions—not least, a Supreme Court that served as a major roadblock to his policy ambitions. His administration tried—unsuccessfully at first—to find ways to design policies that would circumvent the court's reach, and meanwhile to build as much as possible on what already existed, such as social policies adopted by some states. But Obama's policy agenda, in the current political context, has encountered challenges more akin to those faced by Progressive Era reformers, who had to destroy or reconstitute deeply entrenched political relationships if they were to achieve change.[7] For him to meet several of his major policy goals, including those pertaining to health care reform, student aid policy, and the tax system, he could not follow the path of Roosevelt, finding a path *around* political obstacles; rather, he had to find ways to work *through* them, by either obliterating or restructuring them in the process.

THE SUBMERGED STATE

The obstacles to which I am referring are policies that I identify, collectively, as the submerged state: a dense thicket that lies beneath the surface of U.S. market institutions and within the federal tax system. From the perspective of ordinary citizens, these policies have a stealth existence: they function not by sending checks to people, as in the case of Social Security or welfare, or by giving them in-kind benefits, like Food Stamps; rather, they provide incentives and subsidies to private organizations and individuals, encouraging or rewarding them for market activities deemed to serve a public purpose. Contrary to opponents' charges that Obama's agenda involved the usurping by the federal government of private matters, his administration was actually attempting to prune, alter, and reshape these entrenched fixtures of modern governance.

The submerged state has become, over time, a large and formidable structure in the United States. It includes the social tax expenditures that Christopher Howard called "the hidden welfare state," which have grown in number and in real value even in recent decades when some more visible social benefits atrophied in real terms.[8] On net, as of 2008, the amount lost in federal revenues due to social tax breaks was equivalent to 7.4 percent of GDP, up from 4.2 percent in 1976.[9] To put this in perspective, total direct federal spending—on all domestic programs, the military, and interest on the debt—amounts to approximately 18 percent of GDP, making social tax expenditures comparable to between one-third and one-half as much.[10] The submerged state also includes subsidies to private actors, such as student loans, the value of which soared in recent decades as tuition grew and grants withered, inducing students to borrow more and more.

Policies of the submerged state function poorly in terms of guaranteeing economic security and educational opportunity to ordinary Americans. The most expensive ones channel resources especially to the most affluent. For example, the majority of the benefits from the tax-free status of employer-provided retirement benefits and the Home Mortgage Interes Deduction are conferred on households in the top 15 percent of the income distribution.[11] Such policies also channel customers toward particular businesses, thus boosting their profit-making abilities. Sallie Mae, for example, which itself was created by lawmakers in 1973 to encourage student lending, became a private company in 1996 and over the next decade saw the value of its stocks grow by 2,000 percent.[12] Obama was well aware of the ways in which such policies both exacerbate inequality and consume revenues that could otherwise be directed to policies favored by majorities of Americans. Throughout his campaign, he made plans to restructure them. But each of them is guarded by vested interests and stakeholders who benefit from their existence, and who mobilize quickly to defend the status quo.[13] My first point, then, is that Obama took on an especially challenging agenda by prioritizing policies that required reconstitution of existing governance and the confrontation of powerful and entrenched enemies of reform.

Second, and equally important, these policies that Obama sought to reform are largely invisible to most Americans, many of whom barely know they exist—even if they themselves utilize them—and do not understand what is at stake in reforming them. In a national survey I conducted in 2008, I found that those who have utilized submerged state policies do not typically consider government to have aided them— for instance, 60 percent of those who have ever used the Home Mortgage Interest Deduction deny ever having used a government social program. Student loans have long been run primarily through programs in which government subsidizes and guarantees the loans made by banks and lenders, but when beneficiaries were asked about the status of such loans, half reported that they viewed the program as private, while only 43 percent described it as public.[14] Meanwhile, however, as Jacob Hacker has shown, such policies are plainly apparent to the vested interests and stakeholders that benefit from them, and they routinely mobilize quickly and capably to defend the status quo.[15] As a result, the attempt to reform such policies generates a deeply conflictual politics that alienates the public. Combined, these factors mean that the chances of success are slim, and even success may yield limited rewards.

STUDENT AID, TAX EXPENDITURES,
AND HEALTH CARE REFORM

Remarkably, in the realm of student aid, Obama succeeded. For the past two decades, the lenders had become a formidable force, with Washington-based organizations that defended them, and ample resources which they invested in campaign contributions and in lobbying. Their reputation became tarnished in 2007, however, when investigative journalists and New York attorney general Andrew Cuomo revealed that they provided financial aid offices on many college campuses with special incentives in exchange for gaining "preferred lender" status. Then, the financial crisis in 2008 decimated their capacity to make loans, and Congress essentially put them on life support—with government itself providing them with access to capital so that they could continue to make loans. The legislation Obama favored terminated the bank-based system and replaced it entirely with direct loans from government, and redirected the savings to larger Pell grants and other measures aimed to enhance access to college and to raise graduation rates. Despite the lenders' severely weakened capacity, they still held a fair measure of political clout, and Obama's approach would likely have been defeated in the Senate were it not part of the continuing resolution, thus requiring only fifty-one votes for passage.

Yet in keeping with typical efforts to reform the submerged state, even policy success occurred largely under the radar of public awareness. The student aid bill was enacted simultaneously with the health care bill, which stole far more attention throughout the process. The president spoke about it rarely—in only nine public statements in his first fourteen months in office.[16] After he signed the bill, only one in four Americans told pollsters they knew much about it.[17] Ironically, even the implementation of direct lending may continue to cloak government's role, not least because the lenders secured the right to service future loans. The Obama administration does not seem oriented, furthermore, to revealing government's role as it administers such loans: a top official in the U.S. Department of Education said that from the point of view of student borrowers, the experience would be the same as it had been under the bank-based system.[18] Policy delivery may still fail to cultivate among students awareness that it is government that is enabling them to attend college.

The invisibility of policy achievements is highlighted also by Obama's efforts to restructure the tax code. Early on, Obama scored what seemed like victories by including in the 2009 stimulus bill extensive new tax breaks—totaling 37 percent of the $288 billion law—that were aimed primarily to help low- to middle-income families. But those accomplishments, which actually amounted to enlarging the submerged state, would turn out to be the easy part. Gaining credit for it proved elusive: one year later, when pollsters asked whether the Obama administration had raised or lowered taxes for most Americans, only 12 percent of respondents answered correctly that taxes had decreased; 53 percent mistakenly thought taxes had stayed the same, and 24 percent even believed they had increased![19] Meanwhile, in order to finance health care reform, the Obama administration set about attempting to scale back the extent to which wealthy people can benefit from the most expensive tax breaks, but to no avail. Organizations from the National Association of Realtors to the Council on Foundations quickly mobilized in opposition, and members of both parties responded by denouncing such plans. On net, in tax policy, enlarging the submerged state proved relatively easy, but reducing its size and upward redistributive elements all but impossible, except for the limitations in the health care bill on the tax-exempt status of so-called Cadillac plans.

National health insurance for all has been the holy grail of the Democratic Party, long sought after in vain, and policies achieved in the past themselves sometimes functioned as obstacles to attaining it. The system of health coverage that evolved through the mid-twentieth century—Medicare and Medicaid for the elderly and for many of the poor, and government-subsidized, employer-provided health insurance for those who qualified for it—shaped the course of future struggles both by nurturing vested interests and by shaping popular assumptions.[20] Like other aspects of the submerged state, the private health insurance component fostered industries that became politically powerful in protecting their status. It also gave many citizens the impression that health care for working-age adults is an activity that appropriately belongs to the private sector, and it blinded them to the generous support government provides for such coverage.

Unlike in the realm of student aid, the Democrats stood no chance of dismantling the submerged state underlying health care coverage, which still loomed powerful even in the midst of the recession. Instead, it was necessary to negotiate and cut deals with stakeholders, and the Obama administration did so—with the American Medical Association, insurance companies, pharmaceutical companies, and the American Hospital Association, among others. As a result, the legislation that critics on the right termed a "government takeover" in fact possesses features strongly supported by these players, as Skocpol explains in her recent book with Lawrence R. Jacobs, *Health Care Reform and American Politics*. Insurance companies, for example, strongly supported the "individual mandate" feature that would require all Americans to purchase health insurance because it would both deliver to them millions of new customers—aided by tax subsidies—and help create larger risk pools, thus lowering costs.[21] Yet such negotiations disgusted much of the public, as many of them had hoped Obama could transcend the politics of insider deals. The resulting legislation includes not only several forms of visible governance but also expansions of the submerged state, features that may continue to obscure government's role in providing for the nation's health care—despite the substantial role it has played and will continue to play.

Many American citizens who lived through the Great Depression remembered, decades later, how government policies had affected their families in that era. Not all memories were positive: for example, some recalled how relatives who owned small businesses disliked the regulations that the National Industrial Recovery Act imposed. But many described how the Civilian Conservation Corps, the Works Progress Administration, and other relief programs had provided jobs, and how public assistance and unemployment insurance had helped keep them afloat.[22] Americans today, by contrast, have little awareness of Obama's policy achievements because so many are hidden in the submerged state, and people are quite unlikely, decades hence, to be telling of the tax breaks or expanded insurance coverage that aided their families in this period of reform.

Puzzles of Contemporary Political Behavior

Skocpol's fascinating treatment of the Tea Party insurgency prompts me to now consider a few ways in which existing policies and Obama's policy agenda may themselves be influencing the attitudes and rates of participation of Americans who have been mobilized by it, as well as among those who have not. To begin, one of the most riveting puzzles Skocpol raises pertains directly to existing policies, namely, that many of those who claim to want smaller government do actually support continuation of our largest programs, Social Security and Medicare, and in many instances even benefit from them themselves. This paradox prompted me to examine more closely the national survey data I mentioned above, collected in 2008, to probe the views of beneficiaries of these programs. In fact, many of them fail to report that they have ever utilized a government social program: this was the case for 44 percent of Social Security recipients and 40 percent of Medicare recipients.[23] This surprising outcome owes in part to policy design. Although these policies are relatively visible compared to those belonging to the submerged state, still they contain some features that can obscure their status as public social benefits. Roosevelt, hoping to make Social Security sustainable, deliberately planned for it to be financed by payroll taxes and thereby framed as a personal entitlement. Medicare, since the 1970s, has given beneficiaries the option of receiving their benefits through a private health insurance plan; in 2010, 24 percent of beneficiaries—11.1 million people—did so, getting their benefits through an insurance company rather than from government directly.[24] Fewer recipients of these policies appear to think of them when asked about government social program usage than do those who have utilized policies such as Social Security disability, Food Stamps, or welfare—notably, all policies that require beneficiaries to engage in more frequent interaction with government in order to establish or maintain their eligibility status.

Looking more closely, however, my collaborator Julianna Koch and I found that not all beneficiaries of Social Security and Medicare fail to identify their benefits as ones that emanate from government: we found that the visibility of these particular programs—which belong to a group we classify as "partly visible"—depends on the interaction between policy design and beneficiaries' own political attitudes. The most important factor is ideology: comparing two beneficiaries of these same policies, who possess the same personal traits but who differ in their political ideology, the liberal will say that he or she uses a "government social program" whereas the conservative will say that he or she does not. In addition, we find that beneficiaries of these same policies who happen to strongly disapprove of welfare benefits are themselves less likely to admit that they themselves utilize a "government social program"; presumably this is because they associate that term with programs for people they consider "undeserving," and as Skocpol has found, they believe that they themselves are entitled to the policies from which they benefit. These findings show that in today's highly polarized polity, even when people personally experience the same policy, they may interpret its meaning and status differently, understanding it in starkly divergent ways.[25]

Skocpol's discussion of the Tea Party, of citizens whose activism has been ignited by the current political environment, prompts me to wonder more broadly about who is *not* currently mobilized politically: the relatively little grassroots mobilization among progressives is as noteworthy as its abundance among conservatives. The first puzzle this raises is: Why has popular momentum in the midst of the current recession been generated mostly on the right, whereas during the 1930s it occurred primarily on the left? Throughout the Great Depression, maverick populist leaders rallied support among large groups of Americans for greater government involvement in the economy and for redistributive policies. These included Louisiana senator Huey Long, with his "Share Our Wealth" campaign; Father Charles Coughlin, the popular but unpredictable "Radio Priest" whose on-air sermons about social justice lambasted Wall Street; and Francis Townsend, a doctor who energized senior citizens in support of an old-age pension plan that would require beneficiaries to retire and to spend their benefits, on the assumption that it would reduce unemployment and stimulate the economy.[26] During 2009 to 2010, organized labor did rally members in some key states and congressional districts on behalf of health care reform, and in 2011, mass protests emerged in Wisconsin in response to Republican governor Scott Walker's efforts to take away collective bargaining rights of public-sector unions. Aside from these short-lived and localized bursts of activism, however, the present crisis—or perhaps more to the point, Obama's presidency—has given rise primarily to the Tea Party, with its demands for reductions in the size of government and scaling back aid to those it considers "undeserving."

Second, Skocpol's attention to who is mobilized makes me wonder whether or not Obama's presidency will, over time, generate any of the enduring mobilization and partisan allegiance of new and young voters that emerged during Roosevelt's presidency. Kristi Andersen found that the shift toward strong support for Democratic candidates between 1928 and 1936 could not be explained by the "conversion" of Republican voters, as relatively few changed their allegiances. Rather, the Democrats succeeded by mobilizing people who had barely participated previously, predominantly among first- and second-generation immigrants as well as among recently enfranchised women and the young. Once such voters came on board for Democrats, the party successfully retained their support.[27] Obama's election in 2008 was aided by the turnout of many first-time voters—particularly among the young and African Americans—as well as the fact that many Republicans stayed away from the polls.[28] The composition of the electorate helped Obama win the largest margin of victory of any first-term Democratic president since Franklin D. Roosevelt, and to gain control of both chambers for the first time in a presidential election since 1992.[29] Not surprising for a midterm election, 2010 involved a very different electorate, one that was older, was more affluent, and included a higher proportion of whites than the 2008 presidential election had included. The numbers are striking: while 51.1 percent of 18- to 29-year-olds voted in 2008—the third-highest rate since the voting age became 18—only 22.8 percent of that age group turned out in 2010; and whereas 43 percent of the young who voted in 2008 did so for the first time, novices made up only 15 percent of the age group among its 2010 voters.[30] In addition, African Americans declined from 12 percent of the electorate in 2008 to 10 percent in 2010.[31] The question is whether in 2012, when Obama is once again at the top of the ticket, Democrats can once again effectively mobilize constituencies that tend to favor them. The party will still be challenged unless it can make visible to the electorate—through political communication, design, and delivery—the reforms it has achieved, showing how they make a positive difference in citizens' lives.

Reconnecting Citizens to Governance?

Once Congresswoman Ann Marie Buerkle had been in office for a few weeks she returned to the district, fresh from casting her vote to repeal health care reform, and held her first town meeting. At the event she was asked twice about the health insurance she receives. At first she deflected the question, expressing surprise at why constituents were interested, and then she claimed that taxpayers did not pay anything for her health coverage. After a staffer handed her a note, she corrected herself, and explained that like most employees, she pays a contribution toward her insurance but that the government—her employer—pays the rest.[32] The failure of a member of the U.S. Congress herself to recognize government's role in providing for her social benefits only underscores how invisible so many policies and reforms are to ordinary Americans.

For too long, American politics has been dominated by a stale debate between whether government solutions or market solutions function more effectively—rhetoric that has persisted even though both Democrats and Republicans have long endorsed policies that utilize both, in the form of subsidies, tax breaks, and regulations. In his inaugural address, Obama promised to move beyond this false dichotomy, and he has held to his word. Despite enormous economic and political obstacles, he has managed to transform several policies, tilting benefits to working families and the middle class. But to many citizens, it is not clearly apparent what difference these policies make. Such hidden achievements, though significant for their social and economic terms, nonetheless fail to generate broad public support, to motivate voters to go to the polls, or to stimulate the citizen advocacy that could help make them sustainable. Moreover, they permit Americans to overlook or at least to underestimate the role of government in their social provision and to exaggerate that of markets.

When Obama campaigned for the presidency, he set out to "reclaim the meaning of citizenship" and restore the vital trust between people and their government. Achieving these goals will require his administration to find ways, through policy communication, policy design, and policy delivery, to make government's role more apparent to citizens. If this occurs, it will enable people to form opinions about policies that are now obscured from their view and to act politically in response to them. If Obama succeeds in doing so, he will not only strengthen his presidency; more importantly, he will help to revitalize American democracy.

5

MAKING SENSE OF AMERICA'S
POLITICAL MAELSTROM

Theda Skocpol

P ROBING THE CROSS-CURRENTS OF U.S. POLITICS AT this juncture of economic crisis, rising social tensions, and extreme partisan polarization is quite a challenge. As the 2011 Alexis de Tocqueville lecturer, I have been fortunate to be joined in this endeavor by three skilled and thoughtful fellow analysts, each with his or her own take on what has happened through the electoral swings of 2008 and 2010, and each with a unique sense of what may come next as the United States careens into another pivotal moment of clashing visions and voter verdicts in 2012.

Political scientist Larry Bartels draws on a wealth of data and knowledge about the long-term dynamics of U.S. elections to argue that Obama and the 111th Congress of 2009 and 2010 accomplished about what they could in terms of policy shifts—and indeed provoked the electoral backlashes mainstream political scientists would predict when they pushed beyond the sorts of modest governmental steps regular Americans were prepared to accept. Obama should have attempted even less than he did, Bartels seems to say; and he certainly disagrees with my argument that Obama needed a more robust, publicly explained strategy to promote jobs and economic growth. Mickey Edwards offers the unique perspective of a former congressional leader and a participant in the moderate wing of the Republican Party. He holds that the Tea Party's reaction against Obama's reforms has been overplayed, and attributes such political backlash as the president and congressional Democrats got in 2010 to average voter disillusionment with the content of the president's program. Finally, Suzanne Mettler thinks deeply and in innovative ways about how the "submerged" characteristics of America's public social policies—the various programs and tax breaks that add up to our version of the welfare state—shape citizen perceptions of what government has done, or might do, to influence people's lives for better or worse. She deploys her theory and data to help explain why Obama's reformist policy accomplishments have not been readily visible to citizens who benefit from them, and to explain why partisans of the right and left may view the same policies and reforms very differently.

Each commentator has astute things to say about the current political juncture and what may come next; and each raises telling questions about the analysis I have offered about the accomplishments and fumbles of the early Obama administration and the political reactions of citizens and rival politicians. I cannot do full justice to all that each commentator has to offer, but I will take this opportunity to respond to key points from each, highlighting expectations for 2012 as well as analyses of what happened between 2008 and 2010.

Was Obama as Reformer Doomed to Provoke Political Backlash?

Larry Bartels is visibly irritated at leftist commentators such as Robert Kuttner, who wanted President Barack Obama to use the bully pulpit of the presidency from the start to demonize Wall Street and push for aggressive government-led restructuring of the economy. At times, it almost seems as if Bartels wants me to take Kuttner's position; he speaks of me as a "progressive," even though my Tocqueville lecture is meant as social science analysis, not political advocacy. For the most part, Bartels realizes that I use the New Deal analogy as a historical comparison, not as a normative call to arms.

Bartels and I agree on most of the ways in which Franklin Roosevelt and Barack Obama faced very *different* political challenges and opportunities. Comparisons across political time—between two instances in which reform-oriented Democratic presidents backed by congressional majorities arrive in office during national economic crises—can be very useful for highlighting differences as well as similarities. Bartels acknowledges key differences—such as the depth of the jobs crisis by the time FDR took office, versus Obama's arrival just as employment contractions were accelerating—but he also stresses similarities. He is right, for example, to point out that FDR, like Obama, had many disappointed friends as well as dedicated political enemies. My analysis is not meant to question that; rather I am asking why Obama's enemies were so quick to mobilize virtually unanimous and highly effective obstruction in Congress, and why they proved so effective in mischaracterizing and demonizing Obama's successfully enacted legislative reforms, such as the American Recovery and Reinvestment Act and the Patient Protection and Affordable Care Act.

Bartels comes from a wing of the political science profession that assumes basic continuity of processes across vast stretches of time, while I come from an institutional-historical school of thought that looks for ways in which electoral processes and developments in public opinion are conditioned by large-scale changes in surrounding institutions—such as changes in the structure of mass media. In stressing similarities between the 1930s and 1960s, Bartels looks for what seem to be normal swings in public opinion and electoral fortunes. He suggests that Democrats naturally experienced huge setbacks in the 2010 midterm elections because the public was disillusioned with the overly ambitious reforms they enacted—especially health care reform. And he invokes FDR's reelection in 1936 following upswings in disposable income for ordinary Americans to imply, very strongly, what mainstream political scientists all believe: that Obama is virtually toast in 2012, that he cannot be reelected given the adverse income trends most Americans are experiencing.

Bartels and others in political science may turn out to be right about Obama versus Whatever Republican in 2012. I argued that widespread public disillusionment with the sluggish economic recovery was the predominant force behind Democratic losses in 2010, and I have no doubt that similar public concerns will drag Obama down in 2012. But I find it interesting that Bartels does not invoke any comparison between 1934 and 2010—the first midterm elections faced by the reformist Democratic presidents and their parties once they took office amid deep and protracted economic crises. FDR and the Democrats did not preside over any quick economic recovery in 1933 and 1934, but they nevertheless gained rather than lost congressional seats in 1934. Obama and the Democrats almost certainly did at least as much to buoy a sagging economy in 2009 and 2010 as Democrats did back in 1933 and 1934. Yet Democrats experienced massive losses in 2010, far beyond normal swings against an in-party in hard times.

Bartels—and in this he is joined by Mickey Edwards—seems to attribute the extraordinary size of congressional losses for Democrats in 2010 to the supposed unpopularity of Obama's Affordable Care Act (plus the House Democratic vote for environmental legislation). Obama's health reform was "too ambitious" for most Americans to support, Bartels argues. But this follows the usual political science approach to public policy, ignoring altogether both the content of public policy and the ways in which its features are, or are not, made visible to the public. My approach, by contrast, takes the content of policy very seriously, and shines the spotlight on the political and institutional features, as well as strategic decisions, that affect how voters, and potential voters, understand or misunderstand policy issues.

The Affordable Care Act of 2010 was, by all objective accounts, an extremely moderate piece of reform legislation. Its central features—new "exchanges" and subsidies to encourage the purchase of private insurance, along with new rules for private insurance plans—were adopted from plans once put forward by the right-wing Heritage Foundation and were modeled closely on the Massachusetts health insurance reforms championed and designed by Republican Mitt Romney. The actual legislative processes leading to the enactment of Affordable Care catered repeatedly to the policy preferences of a handful of centrist Republicans and Democrats. As for public opinion, the best attitude surveys—such as those conducted repeatedly over many months by the Kaiser Family Foundation—show overwhelming public approval for almost all the specific provisions actually in the

Affordable Care Act. Not just Democrats but also Independents and Republicans approve of new rules for insurance companies; subsidies to make health insurance affordable for small businesses and families of modest means; transparent new "health exchanges" to allow comparison shopping; improvements in Medicare prescription drug coverage; and new rules allowing young adults to stay on family health insurance plans to age 26. Public opinion surveys also show that a substantial portion of Americans who say they, in general, "disapprove" of the Affordable Care say this because they thought the law should have done more, not because they consider it overly "ambitious"!

Given that the general public strongly approves of virtually everything actually in the Affordable Care Act, how can we say that Democrats lost a surplus of seats in 2010 simply because they voted for this reform? We cannot, unless we are practicing a very superficial kind of political science—where both the size of the vote and superficially measured reasons are tossed into a regression equation. This just is not good enough. We have to probe more deeply and ask the questions I asked: How did reduced voter turnout in 2010 compared to 2008 hurt the president's efforts? In what ways did Tea Party mobilizations focused on older, white, economically comfortable voters contribute to the negative views of such voters about health reform overall, and to the lopsided victories the GOP registered in the low-turnout elections in 2010 in which many Democrats stayed home? We might still conclude that Affordable Care was a high-stakes reform to pursue headed into a midterm election in which the segments of the population it was designed to help—younger, minority Americans—were the least likely to vote. But we would arrive at this conclusion only after moving beyond vague—and misleading—labels about "ambitious" versus moderate reforms.

We also need to ask about public perceptions of policy initiatives—and how they are shaped in historically specific institutional and political circumstances. In 2009 and 2010, what about the structure of the media and the partisan atmosphere made it so easy for the GOP—and Tea Party forces—to mischaracterize and demonize health reform? To profoundly mischaracterize a relatively moderate reform with many specific elements that most Americans approve? And how did the process by which reform was debated and formulated become so protracted, messy, and contentious—even when, as repeatedly happened, the president and leading Democrats acceded to specifics Republicans had long championed? Considerable evidence exists to suggest that public opinion on health reform soured as the process dragged on and tawdry compromises were made to attract marginal votes in the Senate. How could we possibly understand what happened without highlighting the GOP leadership's choices, their deliberate decision to obstruct, polarize, and use the filibuster to delay every step? Republicans in the 111th Congress chose *not* to join in governance and make compromises. I highlight and seek to explain why those choices were made, and why they could work so well for the obstructionists.

Bartels suggests that leftists—unnamed—were responsible for the protracted effort to enact Affordable Care because they insisted "too long" on the public option. I do not think there is much evidence for that. Legislative efforts were dragged out, especially in the Senate, over efforts to attract moderate Republican support in the summer and fall of 2009. Those efforts hardly paid off at all, and the reason was that GOP congressional leaders, bolstered by Tea Party protesters and funders, persuaded formerly middle-of-the-road GOP senators like Senator Grassley that compromise would be political suicide for them. All-out Republican obstruction was much more responsible for the protracted and messy legislative process about health reform than anything leftists inside or outside Congress did or could do. My analysis goes more deeply than the usual superficial regression studies or vague claims about contentless policy because we need to know much more about how partisan warfare and political miscommunication work in our time to comprehend what happened here.

To pinpoint his strongest critique, Bartels takes sharp issue with my mild criticism of Obama's public leadership on the economy, dismissing my claim that Obama and his team would have done better if, from the start, they had focused on job creation rather than placing an emphasis only on stopping the financial meltdown and goosing aggregate economic growth. I also maintain that Obama and his team needed to more fully and consistently explain to the public how the American Recovery and Reinvestment Act was designed to work. Because they never did this in a high-profile way, they left the field clear for GOP leaders and conservative ideologues to demonize and undermine the president's recovery strategy. Of course, GOP critics had an entire media sector, Fox and friends, to get their message out.

My analysis in this area is admittedly speculative. Bartels may be right in his claim that President Obama did and said all he could to promote economic recovery, and he and I certainly agree that Congress as it operated in 2009 would not have passed a larger spending measure as such. Nevertheless, at the level of presidential communication, the contrast to FDR in his first two years is quite clear. FDR did not successfully bring about any quick recovery either, but he did present himself to ordinary Americans as obsessively focused on job creation, and avoided any sense that he was all about bailing out Wall Street. FDR self-consciously attempted to shape public understanding of what he was trying to do economically, and his efforts likely bolstered the fortunes of Democrats in 1934. Similarly, amid an economic downturn in the early 1980s, President Ronald Reagan did a good job of convincing the public that he had a viable economic recovery strategy compared to his political opponents, and his party escaped electoral disaster in a dicey midterm election.

Obama has struggled with a financial crisis that involves prolonged deleterious effects on economic growth and family incomes, so much of the problem has to do with the nature of the economic downturn and the timing of his arrival in office. Nonetheless, Obama could have vociferously championed specific job creation measures understandable to ordinary people. He might even have been better off reducing the omnibus "stimulus" and continuing to push for waves of investments in concrete public goods, such as highways, universal Internet access, and bridge repairs. Such investments were there in the American Recovery and Reinvestment Act, but they got buried in a whole that was all too easy for Republicans to demonize as part of the previous "Wall Street bailout." When Obama finally made the shift to pressing for specific, popular job-creation measures in the late summer of 2011, his political fortunes compared to those of Republicans in Congress started to improve. And so did the political fortunes of congressional Democrats compared to those of the congressional GOP. All that I have claimed is that President Obama and his economic and political teams should have started communicating about job creation as a priority in January 2009, not in September 2011. They should have done this regardless of what could pass Congress at any given time because shaping the public's sense of who is trying to do what and who is obstructing positive efforts at job creation has always been important. Citizen understanding is just as important as expert policy.

Is the Tea Party Overblown?

To make sense of what is happening in U.S. politics today, Mickey Edwards draws in fascinating ways on his experiences as a Republican representative and member of the House leadership in the 1980s. From his own experience alongside President Reagan, Edwards knows that it is all too easy for a partisan congressional majority to overread election victories as a sweeping mandate to shift, wholesale, the direction of public policy. Like Bartels, Edwards correctly underlines that American voters are often of mixed mind and tend to be wary of any initiatives they consider big and sudden. Yet amid deepening ideological and partisan polarization, especially in Congress, representatives can be tempted to "go big" even after winning by narrow margins. Edwards points to ways in which this tendency has become more pronounced over time, as primary election challenges and the gerrymandering of safe House districts deepen the disconnect between middle-of-the-road public opinion and the policy preferences of politicians elected to the House of Representatives.

Edwards is certainly correct that we regularly see a measure of partisan overreach in Congress. But I think Edwards underestimates the degree to which partisan polarization has, for years, been skewed toward the right. And he certainly underestimates the degree to which the House GOP shifted to the very far right after the 2010 midterm elections. As quantitative measures of congressional tendencies have nailed down, Democrats remain a mix of moderates and liberals, but Republicans—especially in the House, but also in the Senate and in the ranks of presidential contenders for 2012—nowadays skew very sharply toward the extreme right. They adopt policy stands that simply do not reflect mainstream public opinion.

For many years, ideological advocacy groups—such as the Club for Growth and Grover Norquist's antitax advocacy group—have been adept at using big-money contributions in Republican primaries to enforce extreme antitax orthodoxy on GOP officeholders and candidates, who fear these money-wielding elites more than they fear the so-called median voter. After 2008, this rightward tilt in Republican Party politics became even more extreme with the advent of the Tea Party, which I have argued marries grassroots activism to big-money funders and professional policy-pushers determined to re-make the Republican Party as a hard-right, antigovernment, take-no-prisoners operation.

The forces pushing against bipartisan compromise that worry Mickey Edwards when he looks back at the 1980s and 1990s have only gained strength and ferocity of late. As spelled out in my discussion of the Tea Party here (and in my new book with Vanessa Williamson on *The Tea Party and the Remaking of the Republican Conservatism*), there is over-whelming empirical evidence that President Obama faces extreme, unusually uncompromising Republican opposition. Mickey Edwards, bless him, is far too hopeful when he opines that Tea Partiers might be just run-of-the-mill small-government conservatives. His misjudges the Tea Party–supported Republicans who took office in Congress in 2011 and in statehouses such as those in Wisconsin, Maine, and Florida. Many of these Tea Party–oriented GOP officeholders are determined to destroy much of what government does, including Social Security programs and regulations supported by large majorities of Americans. Tea Party–oriented GOPers in Congress have been willing to push the federal government to the brink of catastrophic default, and block an array of job-creation measures, in order to express their hostility toward President Obama and further their aim of deconstructing much of the federal government. There is nothing run of the mill about Tea Party extremism in or out of office.

That brings me, finally, to Edwards's take on President Obama himself. Edwards rightly points out that the president is well liked personally, even by the considerable swathes of the public who distrust his policies. As Obama tacked toward "the middle" after the Democratic defeats in November 2010, he regained some public support, Edwards suggests; and he believes a more cautious and moderate Obama may prove successful in his bid for reelection in 2012.

At a general level, public opinion surveys show that Obama, like Ronald Reagan, is more personally popular than policy positions alone would dictate. But here again, I think we need to pay more careful attention to the true content of policies, and ask why, at times, there is such a gap between what people tell survey researchers about their general reactions—for example, to "health reform" or to the "Obama jobs bill" overall—and what they say when asked about the specific content of those policies. Not only is Obama as a person more popular than public images of his policies. The specific, true provisions of his policies are also more popular than the overall labels of those policies!

Noting public approval of President Obama's triumphs in fighting terrorism and killing Bin Laden, Edwards believes that 2012 may prove more propitious for Obama than 2010, especially because more voters will turn out and the president himself will be front and center. True enough, but the evidence remains clear that debates during the 2012 elections include issues of economic growth, job creation, and the mix of taxes and spending cuts that should go into improving the long-term federal budget. The Tea Party–backed GOP has backed Obama into a corner in a number of these areas, by overtly blocking any congressional actions that would settle budget issues and stimulate economic growth.

It has become unmistakably clear that the Republican Party in Congress is determined to obstruct effective governance in pursuit of a strategy of removing Obama in 2012—indeed, in the hope that the GOP can win across-the-board victories in the House, Senate, presidency, and many statehouses. Should the Tea Party–backed GOP achieve such sweeping 2012 victories and proceed to take extreme and sudden policy steps, Edwards's worries about overreach would again come true. The general public would quickly sour on Republican extremism—and probably much more thoroughly than they soured on Democrats after 2008. Repealing Affordable Care will not turn out to be popular when it is actually done; nor will eviscerating Medicare or slashing student aid or shrinking Medicaid.

Still, across-the-board GOP victories in 2012 may not actually happen. As Edwards rightly points out, Obama has reservoirs of personal popularity to draw upon. What is more, Tea Party–backed Republicans are losing public approval.

And a presidential contest changes the possibilities for communicating with the general public. As a candidate for re-election, President Obama has new chances to explain the actual content of major legislation such as Affordable Care and the regulation of financial institutions; and he can draw clear contrasts between his economic, social, and tax policies and those favored by Republicans.

Can Obama Make Reform Popular in a Presidential Year?

This brings us to Suzanne Mettler's compelling analysis of the myriad ways in which the accumulated policies of America's "submerged state" contributed to the paradoxical results of Obama's early presidency. The paradox is put even more crisply by Mettler than I managed to do myself: "How could Obama achieve so much of his policy agenda, and yet fail to reap political benefits from it?" As we have seen, both Bartels and Edwards tend to think the puzzle is not so puzzling because, they suggest, Obama and the Democrats of the 111th Congress overreached—pushed unpopular reforms or attempted more ambitious reforms than the public was prepared to support. I have questioned these arguments, especially where health care reform was concerned. Not only was the content of the Affordable Care Act remarkably moderate—to the right of what Republican President Nixon favored in the 1970s—the specific features of the law enacted are almost all widely popular. Suzanne Mettler goes further than I have done, however, to probe the nature of the inherited policy realms in which Obama and his allies sought to enact reforms.

Back in the 1930s, FDR and his allies proposed and at times enacted new forms of government intervention in the economy, labor markets, and social life. What they wanted to do was usually highly visible to potential supporters and opponents alike. There were enormous obstacles, to be sure, and as Mettler aptly puts it, the New Dealers had to work around those obstacles. For example, they had to find ways to neutralize conservative southern Democratic opposition to many new measures. In a number of cases they did this simply by leaving economic sectors centered in the white-dominated South out of coverage of new federal labor regulations and social programs. Social Security, for instance, originally left out employees in agriculture, in large part to blunt the opposition of white southerners to providing any kind of welfare benefits to African Americans.

But, as Mettler details, decades later President Obama and his allies tackled promising—and potentially very popular—reforms in health insurance, student aid, and other realms against a backdrop of dense, long-accumulated federal regulations and subsidies in those realms. The Obamites had to work through thickets, not go around them. And the thickets they had to hack their way through had often grown up under Democratic as well as Republican sponsorship. Arguably, the enactment of Medicare and Medicaid in the mid-1960s, when liberal Democrats briefly held the presidency and congressional majorities, was the last time that highly visible government benefits were added to the U.S. welfare state inherited from the 1930s. Since the 1970s and 1980s, liberals have made all kinds of compromises with moderates and conservatives opposed to direct tax-and-spend social programs. They have fashioned tax credits and regulations to induce private actors to provide social benefits indirectly, often subsidizing business profits at the same time help is delivered to middle-class Americans. Student loans are a good case in point. For years, the federal government guaranteed profits to private lenders in return for their willingness to extend and administer college loans, wasting large amounts of taxpayer money in the process. College loans looked to families and students as if they were "private," but actually the government made them possible and guaranteed banks against loan defaults.

In her pathbreaking new book *The Submerged State: How Invisible Government Policies Undermine American Democracy,* Mettler details the many similar kinds of regulations, tax breaks, and indirect forms of social provision that have accumulated in recent decades. In her commentary here, she spells out the consequences for Barack Obama and his allies when they arrived in office in 2009, promising to redirect taxes, regulations, and spending to do more to help lower- and middle-income Americans. In policy realms such as health care and college loans, Obama attempted to reduce tax breaks that subsidize business profits and favor the wealthiest Americans, in order to free up resources to help ordinary Americans. His administration also proposed lots of new subsidies and regulations designed to aid the middle class and the less privileged. Each Obama reform effort looked good on paper, but in political practice it involved stepping on the toes of powerful political actors who clearly understood what they have to lose, while promising benefits that are too obscure or indirect for most citizens to understand.

Mettler relates in vivid detail the telling story of student loan reform in the Obama presidency. In a truly remarkable triumph, Obama and the Democrats in Congress managed to eliminate the profit-seeking banker middlemen and improve college loan terms for middle-class families and beef up spending for government-administered Pell grants to needy college students. They helped young people, a key Obama constituency. But much of what they accomplished is not very visible, in part because the endgame got folded into the final legislation for the Affordable Care Act and there was little publicity about the landmark college loan reforms of 2010. But the larger problem, as Mettler explains, was that Obama and his allies executed modifications within "submerged state" subsidies that had never seemed like direct government assistance to many of the recipients in the first place. In many ways, college students and their families may not even realize how much more help they have gotten, or might get, from Obama's reforms. And the same is certainly true for the Affordable Care Act—many of whose promised benefits for low- and middle-income Americans will be indirectly delivered, and are scheduled to kick in only after 2012.

A similarly obscure Obama reform happened in tax policy, with the structural dilemmas exacerbated by the sorts of advice mainstream economists are likely to give a president these days. Obama campaigned for the presidency promising to eliminate the Bush tax breaks for the wealthy, while reducing taxes on Americans making less than a quarter of a million dollars a year. When citizens hear this plan clearly, they approve by large majorities. In practice, Obama did not manage to put a stop to the Bush tax cuts for the rich, but his administration did propose, and Congress did enact, significant tax relief for the vast majority of Americans. But if a tax cut for the majority happens without people knowing, is it really a tax cut?

As the Obama tax reforms took hold, Americans were told in the right-wing media that "Obama increased taxes." And the subtle nature of key changes made it hard for citizens to understand what really was happening. Key tax reductions, for instance, happened by trimming payroll taxes, putting a bit more each month into each employee's regular paychecks. Obama's economic advisors told him to structure the "Making Work Pay" tax cut that way, rather than giving a visible lump-sum refund that could be loudly announced to voters. The economists argued that slight increases in monthly pay would be more likely to be spent, and thus would stimulate the economy, while a lump sum might be saved by thrifty lower-income families. This may make sense in an Ivy League classroom (which is where I heard one of Obama's former advisors make the argument). But in the real world, most of the regular Americans who got the benefit of the Making Work Pay tax cut never knew help had arrived—and could not give credit where credit was due. Most Americans ended up telling pollsters that Obama had either raised taxes or left them unchanged—depriving President Obama and congressional Democrats of the political credit they deserved and needed. What is more, the policy itself did not survive the arrival of Republicans in control of the House of Representatives starting in 2011.

The example of the Making Work Pay tax cut shows, in short, that Obama's team not only struggled with the inherited liabilities of the submerged state—where policies are visible to powerful privileged actors, but invisible to the citizen majority—they actually embraced "submerged" policy-making as the best course of action, especially in their economic recovery efforts. As my Tocqueville lecture argues, Obama's original approach to economic recovery was heavy on insider, expert-fashioned moves that were never explained or made visible to ordinary Americans. So regular voters could not track what was attempted, or accomplished. This is a problem in a democracy. As Suzanne Mettler shows, democratic leadership and public policymaking must be accompanied by citizen comprehension if they are to have any chance of "working" in the sense of building rational majority support. The early Obama presidency focused too much on what was supposed to work technically, and paid too little attention to communicating effectively with the broad citizenry. Policy reforms have to be designed in ways that make broad citizen understanding possible. And their features have to be spelled out through truthful, powerful, and unremitting strategies of public communication.

Mettler ends on a hopeful note about what Barack Obama may be able to do during the 2012 presidential campaign—a campaign that promises to force all players to lay out very clearly what they propose to do about national economic growth, job creation, health care reform, and taxes. Presidential campaigns can be about personalities, and no doubt this one will be to some extent. Americans like Barack Obama personally, and he will do fine in comparison to the GOP contender. Presidential campaigns are also, to a considerable degree, referendums on the economy. Here Obama is in trouble. Even if majorities of Americans still blame George W. Bush rather than Barack Obama for our persistent economic difficulties—and even if majorities have a bit more faith in Obama and the Democrats than in Republicans to fix the problems—Obama is bound to be hurt by the deep public disillusionment about what Washington has done, or might do, to revive growth and jobs. He is the incumbent and he may well go down in 2012 just because a sliver of voters in the middle will say, I like him but his stewardship of the economy has not worked, so let's give the Republican a chance.

But it is also true that a presidential campaign involves many more voters paying attention to what the contenders say. Barack Obama has another opportunity to explain what he wants to do about the economy and jobs—an opportunity he has been taking advantage of since late 2011, with unremitting arguments on behalf of the "American Jobs Act" he has proposed, but which congressional Republicans will not pass. In addition, Obama's health reform is sure to be front and center during the summer and fall of 2012—and he will be able to stress the specific things it does, almost all of them popular, and raise the evident threat of all those things going away, or never coming to fruition, if his Republican opponent takes the White House. Republicans have deliberately polarized the debate over a moderate health reform that does many concretely popular things. Obama will have the opportunity to make them pay for that. Obama is also able to highlight the trade-offs that come from tax breaks for the rich. Americans will hear not just about the wonders of tax cuts in general, but about what the country will have to cut in Social Security and Medicare and other benefits for regular families if Republicans prevail and not only continue but actually increase tax breaks for the very wealthy.

During the first half of his term, Obama, as I have argued, did champion and in part accomplish a genuine "new New Deal" of sorts. He and fellow Democrats paid a short-term electoral price, but in very difficult circumstances, they set in motion important new directions in U.S. economic and social policy, directions that deliver a bit more public support to the majority and ask the wealthy to grab less of the total

U.S. economic and fiscal pie. Obama's political enemies know this, which is why they want him out of office, unable to consolidate and build upon the reforms he has started.

Obama's challenge in 2012 is certainly to convince Americans that he has better ideas about economic growth and job creation than his opponents have. But Obama's challenge is also to let his actual and potential supporters see what he has accomplished since 2008, and convince them that his nascent reforms in education, health care, and beyond are worth fighting for. Obama's reforms may have been fashioned by thrashing through a gnarled forest of inherited tax credits and hidden subsidies, pruning and changing the contours of the submerged state rather than replacing it root and branch. Obama could not start anew, he had to work with inherited policies—and as a result, he often took steps that beneficiaries and potential political supporters can hardly see or understand. But a presidential election year allows—and forces—Obama to make the case for what he has done, as well as what he wants to do. Obama has another opportunity to explain to the majority of Americans what may be lost if he is tossed from office—by shining a bit more light on the pivotal reforms he has achieved and championed in taxes and social benefits. If Americans see and understand the specifics, all the evidence we have suggests that most will approve.

NOTES

1. Obama's New Deal, Tea Party Reaction, and America's Political Future

1. Peter Beinart, "The New Liberal Order," *Time,* November 24, 2008, pp. 30–32.
2. State-level results are discussed in Larry J. Sabato, ed., *Pendulum Swing* (Boston: Longman, 2011), pp. 24–29.
3. A full analysis of what the early Obama administration attempted and achieved in major domestic policy areas appears in Theda Skocpol and Lawrence R. Jacobs, eds., *Reaching for a New Deal: Ambitious Governance, Economic Meltdown, and Polarized Politics in Obama's First Two Years* (New York: Russell Sage Foundation, 2011). This book draws from the introductory chapter of *Reaching for a New Deal* and relies on evidence in the detailed chapters about various policy realms.
4. Timothy F. Geithner, "Welcome to the Recovery," *New York Times,* August 2, 2010.
5. For a sample of this debate as it reached a peak leading into the 2010 elections, see Eric Alterman, "Kabuki Democracy: Why a Progressive Presidency Is Impossible, for Now," *The Nation,* July 7, 2010, pp. 11–14; Michael Hirsh, "Obama's Old Deal: Why the 44th President Is No FDR—and the Economy Is Still in the Doldrums," *Newsweek,* August 29, 2010; John B. Judis, "The Unnecessary Fall: A Counter-History of the Obama Presidency," *The New Republic,* August 12, 2010; and "Defending 'The Unnecessary Fall of Barack Obama,'" *The New Republic,*

August 25, 2010; Ezra Klein, "If Only Obama Had . . . ," *Washington Post* blog, August 19, 2010, http://voices.washingtonpost.com/ezra-klein; Robert Kuttner, *A Presidency in Peril: The Inside Story of Obama's Promise, Wall Street's Power, and the Struggle to Control our Economic Future* (White River Junction, VT: Chelsea Green Publishing, 2010); Charles Krauthammer, "Obama's Next Act," *Washington Post,* July 16, 2010, p. A19; Paul Krugman, "The Pundit Delusion," *New York Times,* July 19, 2010.

6. Chuck Todd and Sheldon Gawiser, *How Barack Obama Won: A State-by-State Guide to the Historic 2008 Presidential Election* (New York: Vintage, 2009).

7. Ibid.; Rob Runyan, "Vote Might Widen Divide between Parents and Children," *USA Today,* November 1, 2008.

8. Stephen Skowronek, *The Politics Presidents Make: Presidential Leadership from John Adams to Bill Clinton* (Cambridge, MA: Belknap Press of Harvard University Press, 1993).

9. Robert Kuttner, "Obama's Economic Opportunity," *The American Prospect* 20, no. 1 (2009): 13–14.

10. Barack Obama, "The American Promise," Acceptance Speech at the Democratic National Convention, Denver, Colorado, August 28, 2008.

11. Lawrence R. Jacobs and Theda Skocpol, eds., *Inequality and American Democracy* (New York: Russell Sage Foundation, 2005); Larry M. Bartels, *Unequal Democracy: The New Gilded Age* (Princeton, NJ: Princeton University Press, 2008), chs. 1–2; Jacob S. Hacker and Paul Pierson, *Winner-Take-All Politics: How Washington Made the Rich Richer—and Turned Its Back on the Middle Class* (New York: Simon and Schuster, 2010), ch. 1.

12. Todd and Gawiser, *How Barack Obama Won,* pp. 30–31.

13. Lloyd A. Free and Hadley Cantril, *The Political Beliefs of Americans: A Study of Public Opinion* (New York: Simon and Schuster, 1968); Benjamin I. Page and Lawrence R. Jacobs, *Class War? What Americans Really Think about Economic Inequality* (Chicago: University of Chicago Press, 2009).

14. Jonathan Alter, *The Promise: Obama, Year One* (New York: Simon and Schuster, 2010), pp. 135–137.

15. See Skocpol and Jacobs, *Reaching for a New Deal,* for analysis of the legislative or administrative means by which Obama's administration pursued policy goals during 2009 and 2010. Administrative means were emphasized in areas such as labor relations where it was impossible to assemble winning coalitions for legislation.

16. James T. Patterson, *Congressional Conservatism and the New Deal* (Lexington: University of Kentucky Press, 1967), ch. 1.

17. Alter, *Promise,* pp. 9–14.

18. Ibid., pp. 49–53.

19. Ibid., p. 206.

20. Paul Krugman, "The Pundit Delusion," *New York Times,* July 19, 2010. For a later retrospect, see Krugman, "The Mistake of 2010," *New York Times,* June 2, 2011.

21. Alter, *Promise,* pp. 85–86; Hirsh, "Obama's Old Deal."

22. Alan Silverleib, "Recession Not Over, Public Says," *CNN.com,* September 26, 2010.

23. James Fallows, "The Chart That Should Accompany Every Discussion of Deficits," *National Journal,* May 13, 2011.

24. Nolan McCarty, Keith T. Poole, and Howard Rosenthal, *Polarized Politics: The Dance of Ideology and Unequal Riches* (Cambridge, MA: MIT Press, 2008).

25. Jacob S. Hacker and Paul Pierson, *Off Center: The Republican Revolution and the Erosion of American Democracy* (New Haven, CT: Yale University Press, 2005); Barbara Sinclair, *Party Wars: Polarization and the Politics of National Policymaking* (Norman: University of Oklahoma Press, 2006).

26. Hacker and Pierson, *Off Center;* Bartels, *Unequal Democracy;* Nolan McCarty, "The Policy Effects of Political Polarization," in *The Transformation of American Politics: Activist Government and the Rise of Conservatism,* ed. Paul Pierson and Theda Skocpol (Princeton, NJ: Princeton University Press, 2007), pp. 233–255.

27. Sarah A. Binder and Steven S. Smith, *Politics or Principle: Filibustering in the United States Senate* (Washington, DC: Brookings

Institution Press, 1996); Thomas E. Mann and Norman Ornstein, *The Broken Branch: How Congress Is Failing America and How to Get It Back on Track* (New York: Oxford University Press, 2006).

28. Ezra Klein, "The Rise of the Filibuster: An Interview with Barbara Sinclair," *Washington Post,* September 26, 2009.

29. Ben Frumin and Jason Reif, "The Rise of Cloture: How GOP Filibuster Threats Have Changed the Senate," *TalkingPointsMemo* blog post, January 27, 2010.

30. Nate Silver, "Obama No F.D.R.—Nor Does He Have F.D.R.'s Majority," *FiveThirtyEight* blog post, March 1, 2010.

31. Patterson, *Congressional Conservatism and the New Deal.*

32. David W. Levy and Russell D. Buhite, eds., *FDR's Fireside Chats* (Norman: University of Oklahoma Press, 1993). The book includes an introduction that puts FDR's use of radio in perspective.

33. Richard Wolffe, *Renegade: The Making of a President* (New York: Crown Publishers, 2009).

34. Peter Dreier, "Lessons from the Health-Care Wars," *The American Prospect* 21, no. 4 (2010): 29–34.

35. Markus Prior, *Post-Broadcast Democracy: How Media Choice Increases Inequality in Political Involvement and Polarizes Elections* (New York: Cambridge University Press, 2007); Robert Y. Shapiro and Lawrence R. Jacobs, "Informational Interdependence: Public Opinion and the Media in the New Communications Era," in Shapiro and Jacobs, eds., *The Oxford Handbook of American Public Opinion and Media,* pp. 3–21 (Oxford: Oxford University Press, 2011).

36. For up-to-date data on the segmentation of audiences by political views, see Pew Research Center for the People and the Press, "Beyond Red vs. Blue: The Political Typology," report released May 4, 2011.

37. Peter Dreier and Christopher R. Martin, "How ACORN Was Framed: Political Controversy and Media Agenda Setting," *Perspectives on Politics* 8, no. 3 (September 2010): 761–792.

38. Mark A. Smith, "Economic Insecurity, Party Reputation, and the Republican Ascendance," in *The Transformation of American Politics,* ed. Pierson and Skocpol, pp. 133–159; Mark A. Smith, *The Right Talk: How Conservatives Transformed the Great Society into the Economic Society* (Princeton, NJ: Princeton University Press, 2007).

39. Hacker and Pierson, *Winner-Take-All-Politics,* part 1; Peter Whoriskey, "With Executive Pay, Rich Pull Away from the Rest of America," *Washington Post,* June 18, 2011.

40. Paul Pierson, "The Rise and Reconfiguration of Activist Government," in *The Transformation of American Politics,* ed. Pierson and Skocpol, pp. 19–38.

41. Bartels, *Unequal Democracy;* Hacker and Pierson, *Winner-Take-All-Politics.*

42. Andrea Louise Campbell, *How Policies Make Citizens: Senior Political Activism and the American Welfare State* (Princeton, NJ: Princeton University Press, 2003).

43. Bartels, *Unequal Democracy,* esp. ch. 9; Martin Gilens, "Inequality and Democratic Responsiveness," *Public Opinion Quarterly* 69, no. 5 (2005): 778–796; Hacker and Pierson, *Winner-Take-All-Politics.*

44. Lawrence R. Jacobs and Theda Skocpol, *Health Care Reform and American Politics: What Everyone Needs to Know* (New York: Oxford University Press, 2010).

45. Suzanne Mettler, "Eliminating the Market Middle-Man: Redirecting and Expanding Support for College Students," in, *Reaching for a New Deal,* ed. Skocpol and Jacobs, pp. 105–138.

46. Judith A. Layzer, "Cold Front: How the Recession Stalled Obama's Clean Energy Agenda," in *Reaching for a New Deal,* ed. Skocpol and Jacobs, pp. 321–385.

47. Andrea Louise Campbell, "Paying America's Way: The Fraught Politics of Taxes, Investments, and Budgetary Responsibility," in *Reaching for a New Deal,* ed. Skocpol and Jacobs, pp. 386–421; Alex Hertel-Fernandez and Theda Skocpol, working paper in progress on Democrats and the failure to stop tax cuts for the rich.

48. These issues are dissected in Suzanne Mettler, "The Transformed Welfare State and the Redistribution of Political Voice," in *The Transformation of American Politics,* ed. Pierson and Skocpol, pp. 191–222; Joe Soss, Jacob S. Hacker, and Suzanne Mettler, eds., *Remaking America: Democracy and Public Policy in an Age of Inequality* (New York: Russell Sage Foundation, 2007).

49. Suzanne Mettler, *The Submerged State: How Invisible Government Policies Undermine American Democracy* (Chicago: University of Chicago Press, 2011).

50. The discussion in this section draws upon Vanessa Williamson, Theda Skocpol, and John Coggin, "The Tea Party and the Remaking of Republican Conservatism," *Perspectives on Politics 9,* no. 1 (March 2011): 25–43. I also draw on further research presented in Theda Skocpol and Vanessa Williamson, *The Tea Party and the Remaking of Republican Conservatism* (New York: Oxford University Press, 2012).

51. Dan Balz and Jon Cohen, "Poll Finds Americans Pessimistic, Want Change: War, Economy, Politics, Sour Views of Nation's Direction," *Washington Post,* November 4, 2007; Megan Thee, "Poll: Record High for Wrong-Track Rating," *New York Times,* October 14, 2008; Johanna Neuman, "As Voters Go to the Polls to Pick His Successor, George W. Bush Hits New Low in Approval Rating," *Los Angeles Times,* November 4, 2008.

52. See, for instance, George Packer, "The Fall of Conservatism," *New Yorker,* May 26, 2008.

53. Conservatives involved in the original February 27 Tea Parties hailed from the online networks Top Conservatives on Twitter and Smart Girl Politics; long-standing antitax campaigners including American Spectator, the Heartland Institute, and Americans for Tax Reform; as well as veterans of the mid-2008 "Don't Go" campaign that urged members of Congress to stay in session to lift the moratorium on offshore drilling.

54. For a full analysis and data on the media's role in encouraging and covering the Tea Party upsurge, see Skocpol and Williamson, *Tea Party,* ch. 4.

55. Williamson, Skocpol, and Coggin, "Tea Party," note 15, lists the polls whose results are summed up here.

56. See, for example, the *USA Today*/Gallup poll, March 26–28, 2010 or Winston Group poll, released April 1, 2009.

57. Bruce E. Keith, David B. Magleby, Candice J. Nelson, Elizabeth Orr, Mark C. Westlye, and Raymond E. Wolfinger, *The Myth of the Independent Voter* (Berkeley: University of California Press, 1992).

58. Quinnipiac Poll, March 16–21, 2010: "Generally speaking, do you consider yourself a Republican, a Democrat, an Independent, or what? (If Independent) Do you think of yourself as closer to the Republican party or the Democratic party?" (Republican + Ind lean Rep, 74 percent; Democrat + Ind lean Dem, 16 percent; Independent, 5 percent; Other, 5 percent; DK/NA, 0 percent.) See also Stanley B. Greenberg, James Carville, Jim Gerstein, Peyton M. Craighill, and Kate Monninger, "Special Report on the Tea Party Movement," Democracy Corps, July 19, 2010, http://www.democracycorps.com/strategy/2010/07/special-report-on-the-tea-party-movement/, 2: "86 percent of Tea Party supporters and activists identify with or lean to the Republican Party."

59. Frank Newport, "Tea Party Supporters Overlap Republican Base," Gallup Survey Report, July 2, 2010.

60. CBS News/*New York Times* poll, April 5–12, 2010: "Have you ever been active in a political campaign—that is, have you worked for a candidate or party, contributed money, or done any other active work?" (Yes, 43; No, 56; DK/NA, 1.) The precise question asked in the CBS News/*New York Times* poll is an unusual one; it has not been used in modern polls. The question *was* asked, however, in a sample of American adults in 1960, and only 17 percent claimed to ever have been active in a political campaign. Center for International Studies, Princeton University, March 1960: "Have you ever been active in a political campaign—that is, have you worked for a candidate or party, contributed money, or done any other active work?" (Yes, have been active, 17; No, 81; Don't know/no answer, 2.) More recent questions include a

time limit, typically asking about political activity in the past three or four years, and so are not directly comparable, but the results are similar to the Princeton study results.

61. CBS News/*New York Times* poll, April 5–12, 2010: "Which one of the following television networks do you watch most for information about politics and current events—ABC, CBS, NBC, CNN, FOX News Channel, MSNBC, or don't you watch television news?" (All respondents: ABC, CBS, NBC, 26 percent; CNN, 17 percent; Fox News Channel, 23 percent; MSNBC, 3 percent; Don't watch news, 16 percent; Other, 3 percent; Combination, 11 percent; DK/NA, 1 percent. Tea Party supporters: ABC, CBS, NBC, 11 percent; CNN, 7 percent; Fox News Channel, 63 percent; MSNBC, 1 percent; Don't watch news, 6 percent; Other, 1 percent; Combination, 10 percent; DK/NA, 1 percent.)

62. The following overview draws on the interviews and field research reported in detail in Williamson, Skocpol, and Coggin, "Tea Party," and in Skocpol and Williamson, *Tea Party,* chs. 1 and 2.

63. David Leonhardt, "In the Process, Pushing Back at Inequality," *New York Times,* March 24, 2010, pp. A1 and A19.

64. Amy Gardner, "Gauging the Scope of the Tea Party Movement in America," *Washington Post,* October 24, 2010.

65. See Skocpol and Williamson, *Tea Party,* ch. 3, including figure 3.1.

66. Evidence from interviews and observations presented in ibid., esp. ch. 3, but also throughout.

67. Wesley P. Hester, "Tea Party All Grown Up and Planning for the Future," *Richmond Times-Dispatch,* October 10, 2010.

68. The goals are clear on the websites of the Cato Institute, Americans for Prosperity, and FreedomWorks. See also Jane Mayer, "Covert Operations: The Billionaire Brothers Who Are Waging a War Against Obama," *New Yorker,* August 30, 2010; and Tom Hamburger, Kathleen Hennessey, and Neela Banerjee, "Koch Brothers Now at Heart of GOP Power," *Los Angeles Times,* February 6, 2011.

69. A third Tea Party organization, Tea Party Nation (TPN), is a for-profit group best known for convening a February 2010 "national convention" featuring Sarah Palin as the keynote speaker. TPN has been beset with controversy about its grassroots authenticity. The second TPN convention, slated for July 2010 and deemed a "unity" convention by organizers, was canceled a month beforehand. See Sheila Burke, "Tenn. Businessman Sues Tea Party Nation Leader," *Associated Press,* March 31, 2010.

70. See, for instance, Ryan J. Reilly, "Tea Party Express Spent Almost $600,000 to Support Miller in Alaska Primary," *TPMMuckraker* website, September 21, 2010.

71. Comments and quotes from Martin come from an interview with Vanessa Williamson and John Coggin on March 11, 2010.

72. In their first year of activity, TPP raised about $900,000, mostly in small donations, before receiving a million-dollar donation from a single anonymous donor. It is unclear how much of this money came from FreedomWorks donors, and how much was raised independently. See Kenneth P. Vogel, "A Tea Party Patriots Overhaul," *Politico,* September 20, 2010.

73. Zachary Roth, "FreedomWorks Says Jump, Tea Partiers Ask How High," *TPMMuckraker* website, August 11, 2009.

74. Mayer, "Covert Operations"; Tim Dickenson, "The Lie Machine: The Plot to Kill Health Care Reform," *Rolling Stone,* October 1, 2009.

75. The complex relationship of the Tea Party and the Republican Party is detailed and discussed in Skocpol and Williamson, *Tea Party,* ch. 5.

76. Quantitative indicators of the leap to the right of the GOP House caucus between the 111th and 112th Congresses have been developed by Adam Bonica of Stanford University and appear on his website Ideological Cartography. See "Introducing the 112th Congress," November 5, 2010, at http://ideologicalcartography.com/2010/11/.

77. Harold Meyerson, "Who's Hurt by Paul Ryan's Budget Proposal," *Washington Post,* April 7, 2011; Bruce Bartlett, "Imbalanced Budget: Ryan Givers Wealthy a Free Pass," *Fiscal Times,*

April 7, 2011. Detailed analyses are available from the Center for Budget and Policy Priorities.

78. Jacobs and Skocpol, *Health Care Reform and American Politics,* ch. 5.

79. Opinion on the Affordable Care Act in all of its complexity can be tracked on the website of the Kaiser Family Foundation, http://www.kff.org/.

80. Trends can be tracked at the websites of the Kaiser Family Foundation and Pew Center for People and the Press, http://pewre search.org/. Telling early results appear at Ian Swanson, "HILL POLL: Majority of Voters Reject Medicare Cuts to Reduce Deficits," *The Hill,* May 2, 2011, and Elspeth Reeve, "70% of Tea Partiers Don't Want to Cut Medicare Either," *National Journal,* April 19, 2011.

81. Bill Schneider, "A Taste of Republican Governance," *Inside Politics with Bill Schneider,* Issue 15, June 2011, p. 4, http://www .thirdway.org.

82. Surveys since 2011 have documented the rising unpopularity of the Tea Party. By September 2011, it was more unpopular than President Obama, according to the CNN/ORC poll of September 23–25, 2011.

2. A New Deal Fantasy Meets Old Political Realities

1. The Editors of *The Economist, The New Deal: An Analysis and Appraisal* (New York: Alfred A. Knopf, 1937), p. 147.

2. Theda Skocpol and Lawrence R. Jacobs, eds., *Reaching for a New Deal: Ambitious Governance, Economic Meltdown, and Polarized Politics in Obama's First Two Years* (New York: Russell Sage Foundation, 2011).

3. "The *New* New Deal: What Barack Obama Can Learn from F.D.R.—and What the Democrats Need to Do," *Time,* November 24, 2008.

4. Peter Beinart, "The New Liberal Order," *Time,* November 13, 2008, http://www.time.com/time/magazine/article/0,9171,1858 873,00.html.

5. John B. Judis, "America the Liberal," *The New Republic,* November 19, 2008, http://www.tnr.com/article/america-the-liberal.

6. Robert Kuttner, *Obama's Challenge: America's Economic Crisis and the Power of a Transformative Presidency* (White River Junction, VT: Chelsea Green Publishing, 2008), p. 1.

7. Larry M. Bartels, "Election Debriefing," CSDP Election 2008, November 6, 2008, http://blogs.princeton.edu/election2008/2008/11/election-debriefing.html. Among others, John Sides, "Truths and Myths about the 2008 Election," The Monkey Cage, November 5–6, 2008, http://www.themonkeycage.org/2008/11/.

8. John B. Judis, "The Unnecessary Fall: A Counter-History of the Obama Presidency," *The New Republic,* August 12, 2010, http://www.tnr.com/article/politics/magazine/76972/obama-failure-polls-populism-recession-health-care.

9. Judis, "America the Liberal."

10. Robert Kuttner, "Unequal to the Moment," *American Prospect,* February 9, 2011, http://prospect.org/article/unequal-moment-0.

11. Ibid.

12. Alan S. Blinder and Mark Zandi, "How the Great Recession Was Brought to an End," Princeton University and Moody's Analytics, July 27, 2010, http://www.Economy.com/mark-zandi/documents/End-of-Great-Recession.pdf.

13. YouGov/Polimetrix survey, October 2010. "Do you know anyone who has had their home foreclosed or fallen behind in their mortgage payments in the past year?" Yes, 36 percent; No, 54 percent; Not sure, 9 percent (weighted results) (numbers do not add up to 100 percent because of rounding).

14. Keith Krehbiel, *Pivotal Politics: A Theory of U.S. Lawmaking* (Chicago: University of Chicago Press, 1998).

15. David M. Herszenhorn, "Recovery Bill Gets Final Approval," *New York Times,* February 14, 2009, p. A14.

16. David M. Herszenhorn and Carl Hulse, "Deal Reached in Congress on $789 Billion Stimulus Plan," *New York Times,* February 12, 2009, p. A1.

17. Robert Pear and David M. Herszenhorn, "Republican's Vote Lifts a Health Bill, but Hurdles Remain," *New York Times,* October 14, 2009, p. A1.

18. David M. Herszenhorn and David D. Kirkpatrick, "Lieberman Gets Ex-Party to Shift on Health Plan," *New York Times,* December 15, 2009, p. A1; Robert Pear, "Senate Passes Health Care Overhaul on Party-Line Vote," *New York Times,* December 25, 2009, p. A1.

19. Judis, "Unnecessary Fall."

20. Sheryl Gay Stolberg and David M. Herszenhorn, "Obama Weighs Paring Goals for Health Bill," *New York Times,* January 21, 2010, p. A1; Sheryl Gay Stolberg, Jeff Zeleny, and Carl Hulse, "Health Vote Caps a Journey Back from the Brink," *New York Times,* March 21, 2010, p. A1.

21. David Leonhardt, "In Health Bill, Obama Attacks Wealth Inequality," *New York Times,* March 24, 2010, p. A1.

22. Kuttner, "Unequal to the Moment."

23. Nolan McCarty, "The Politics of the Pop: The Effects of Ideology, Partisanship, and Interest in the Response to the U.S. Finance Crisis and Great Recession," unpublished paper presented at a conference on Government Responses to the Economic Crisis, Russell Sage Foundation, New York, October 2010.

24. Eric McGhee, "Which Roll Call Votes Hurt the Democrats?," The Monkey Cage, November 9, 2010, http://themonkeycage .org/blog/2010/11/09/which_roll_call_votes_hurt_the/.

25. McGhee estimated that congressional Democrats who supported the American Recovery and Reinvestment Act did 2.8 percent worse in 2010, other things being equal. However, a cross-national analysis of economic growth and election outcomes during the Great Recession suggests that the additional GDP growth attributable to the stimulus plan boosted the aggregate Democratic vote share by somewhere between 2.8 percent and 6.2 percent. See Larry M. Bartels, "Ideology and Retrospection in Electoral Responses to the Great Recession," paper prepared for presentation at a conference on "Popular Reactions to the Great Recession," Nuffield College, Oxford, June 24–26, 2011, http:// www.princeton.edu/~bartels/stimulus.pdf.

26. George C. Edwards III, *On Deaf Ears: The Limits of the Bully Pulpit* (New Haven, CT: Yale University Press, 2003).

27. Katherine S. Newman and Elisabeth S. Jacobs, *Who Cares? Public Ambivalence and Government Activism from the New Deal to the Second Gilded Age* (Princeton, NJ: Princeton University Press, 2010), p. 15.

28. V. O. Key Jr., *Public Opinion and American Democracy* (New York: Alfred A. Knopf, 1961), p. 246.

29. Newman and Jacobs, *Who Cares?*, pp. 17–18.

30. Ibid., p. 45.

31. V. O. Key Jr., *Politics, Parties, and Pressure Groups*, 4th ed. (New York: Thomas Y. Crowell, 1958), pp. 578–579; James L. Sundquist, *Dynamics of the Party System*, revised ed. (Washington, DC: Brookings Institution, 1983), p. 214; Angus Campbell, Philip E. Converse, Warren E. Miller, and Donald E. Stokes, *The American Voter* (New York: John Wiley & Sons, 1960), p. 534.

32. Christopher H. Achen and Larry M. Bartels, "Partisan Hearts and Gall Bladders: Retrospection and Realignment in the Wake of the Great Depression," paper prepared for presentation at the Annual Meeting of the Midwest Political Science Association, Chicago, April 7–9, 2005, http://www.princeton.edu/~bartels/depress3.pdf.

33. Ibid.

34. David R. Mayhew, *Electoral Realignments: A Critique of an American Genre* (New Haven, CT: Yale University Press, 2002), p. 161.

35. Editors of *The Economist, New Deal*, pp. 147–149.

4. Obama and the Challenge of Submerged Policies

1. Mark Weiner, "Central New York Environmental Experts, Dan Maffei Criticize Ann Marie Buerkle's Stance on Global Warming," *Post-Standard*, October 14, 2010, http://www.syracuse.com/news/index.ssf/2010/10/central_new_york_environmental.html; John Gizzi, "Lady from Syracuse," *Human Events.com*, http://www.syracuse.com/news/index.ssf/2010/10/central_new_york_environmental.html.

2. Mark Weimer, "How the West Was Won by Ann Marie Buerkle, Causing an Election Day Tossup in the 25th Congressional District," *Post-Standard*, November 7, 2010, http://www.syracuse .com/news/index.ssf/2010/11/how_the_west_was_won_by_ann _ma.html.

3. Shawn Zeller, "Historic Success, at No Small Cost," *CQ Weekly* (January 11, 2010): 112–121, http://library.cqpress.com.proxy.li brary.cornell.edu/cqweekly/weeklyreport111-000003276735.

4. Joseph J. Schatz, "2010 Vote Studies: Presidential Support," *CQ Weekly* (January 3, 2011): 18–24, http://library.cqpress.com .proxy.library.cornell.edu/cqweekly/weeklyreport112 -000003788814.

5. "61% Favor Repeal of Health Care Law," *Rasmussen Reports,* September 20, 2010, http://www.rasmussenreports.com/public _content/politics/current_events/healthcare/september_2010/61 _favor_repeal_of_health_care_law.

6. Karen Orren and Stephen Skowronek, *The Search for American Political Development* (Cambridge, MA: Harvard University Press, 2004), pp. 21, 20.

7. Stephen Skowronek, *Building a New American State: The Expansion of National Administrative Capacity, 1877–1920* (New York: Cambridge University Press, 1982).

8. Christopher Howard, *The Hidden Welfare State: Tax Expenditures and Social Policy in the United States* (Princeton, NJ: Princeton University Press, 1997).

9. Leonard Burman, Eric Toder, and Christopher Geissler, "How Big Are Total Individual Income Tax Expenditures, and Who Benefits from Them?," Discussion Paper No. 31, 2008, The Urban-Brookings Tax Policy Center, http://www.taxpolicycenter .org/UploadedPDF/1001234_tax_expenditures.pdf.

10. U.S. Congressional Budget Office, "A 125-Year Picture of the Federal Government's Share of the Economy, 1950–2075," Long-Range Fiscal Policy Brief No. 1, July 3, 2002, http://www.cbo.gov /ftpdocs/35xx/doc3521/125RevisedJuly3.pdf; U.S. Joint Committee on Taxation, "Estimates of Federal Tax Expenditures for Fiscal Years," various years.

11. In 2004, 69 percent and 55 percent of the benefits from the non-taxable status of retirement benefits and from the Home Mortgage Interest Deduction, respectively, were conferred on Americans with household incomes of $100,000 or more—the top 15 percent of the income distribution. The tax-free nature of employer-sponsored health insurance is slightly less biased, though still 30 percent of the benefit was allocated to families in the top 15 percent of the income distribution. U.S. Census Bureau, "Annual Social and Economic (ASEC) Supplement," 2005, last modified August 28, 2007, http://pubdb3.census.gov/macro/032007/hhinc /new06_000.htm.

12. Bethany McLean, "Sallie Mae: A Hot Stock, a Tough Lender," *CNN Money*, December 14, 2005, http://money.cnn.com/2005 /12/14/news/fortune500/sallie_fortune_122605/index.htm.

13. Jacob S. Hacker, *The Divided Welfare State: The Battle Over Public and Private Social Benefits in the United States* (New York: Cambridge University Press, 2002), ch. 1.

14. Social and Governmental Issues and Participation Study of 2008, Survey conducted by Survey Research Institute, Cornell University. Principal Investigator, Suzanne Mettler.

15. Hacker, *Divided Welfare State*, ch. 1.

16. Suzanne Mettler, "Reconstituting the Submerged State: The Challenges of Social Policy Reform in the Obama Era," *Perspectives on Politics* 8, no. 3 (September 2010): 814.

17. Survey by Pew Research Center for the People and the Press. April 1–April 5, 2010, based on 1,016 telephone interviews.

18. Confidential interview conducted by author, spring 2010, Washington, D.C.

19. CBS News/*New York Times* Poll 2010, February 5–10, "The Tea Party Movement," http://www.cbsnews.com/htdocs/pdf/poll _Tea_Party_021110.pdf. The question read: "So far, do you think the Obama Administration has increased taxes for most Americans, decreased taxes for most Americans, or have they kept taxes the same for most Americans?"

20. Jacob Hacker, "The Historical Logic of National Health Insurance: Structure and Sequence in the Development of British,

Canadian, and U.S. Medical Policy," *Studies in American Political Development* 12 (1998): 57–130.

21. Lawrence R. Jacobs and Theda Skocpol, *Health Care Reform and American Politics: What Everyone Needs to Know* (New York: Oxford University Press, 2010), pp. 67–76.

22. This observation comes from my own interviews with members of the World War II generation, in 1998–1999, and from assignments I gave to undergraduate students in that same period, to interview grandparents about their memories of New Deal–era policies.

23. Mettler, "Reconstituting the Submerged State," p. 809, table 3.

24. Kaiser Family Foundation, "Medicare: Medicare Advantage. Fact Sheet," September 2010, http://www.kff.org/medicare/up load/2052-14.pdf.

25. Julianna Koch and Suzanne Mettler, "Who Perceives Government's Role in Their Lives? How Policy Visibility Influences Awareness of and Attitudes about Social Spending," paper presented at the Annual Meetings of the Midwestern Political Science Association, Chicago, March 31–April 3, 2011.

26. William E. Leuchtenburg, *Franklin D. Roosevelt and the New Deal, 1932–1940* (New York: Harper & Row, 1963), pp. 96–108.

27. Kristi Andersen, *The Creation of a Democratic Majority, 1928–1936* (Chicago: University of Chicago Press, 1979).

28. Michael P. McDonald, "The Return of the Voter: Voter Turnout in the 2008 Presidential Election," *The Forum* 6, no. 4, article 4: 3; Center for Information and Research on Civic Learning and Engagement, "Will Young Voters Turnout for 2010 Midterm Elections?," http://www.civicyouth.org/wp-content/uploads/2010/09 /2010-Midterm-Circle-PR-final.pdf.

29. James W. Ceaser and Daniel DiSalvo, "The Magnitude of the 2008 Democratic Victory: By the Numbers," *The Forum* 6, no. 4, article 8 (2010): 4–7.

30. Emily Hoban Kirby and Kei Kawshima-Ginsberg, "The Youth Vote in 2008," *CIRCLE:* Fact Sheet, http://www.civicyouth.org /PopUps/FactSheets/FS_youth_Voting_2008_updated_6.22.pdf;

CIRCLE Staff, "Young Voters in the 2010 Elections," *CIRCLE: Fact Sheet,* http://www.civicyouth.org/wp-content/uploads/2010 /11/2010-Exit-Poll-Fact-Sheet.-corrected-Nov-10.pdf.

31. Tom Sander, "2010 Voter Turnout Up, but Not for Youth and Blacks," *Social Capital Blog,* http://socialcapital.wordpress.com /2010/11/04/2010-voter-turnout-up-but-not-for-youth-and%C2 %A0blacks/.

32. Marnie Eisenstadt, "Buerkle Learns to Listen," *Post-Standard,* February 4, 2011, p. A-3.

ABOUT THE AUTHORS

THEDA SKOCPOL is the Victor S. Thomas Professor of Government and Sociology at Harvard University.

LARRY M. BARTELS holds the May Werthan Shayne Chair in Public Policy and Social Science at Vanderbilt University.

MICKEY EDWARDS is Vice President of the Aspen Institute. He was a Republican member of Congress from Oklahoma for sixteen years (1977–1992).

SUZANNE METTLER is the Clinton Rossiter Professor of American Institutions at Cornell University.

INDEX